THE RETURN OF JESUS CHRIST TO PLANET EARTH

JOHN MARINELLI

Fighting The Good Fight of Faith
Copyright © 2023 John Marinelli
Ocala, Florida …All rights reserved.

First Edition: 5/2023

Print ISBN: 978-1-0879-1506-7
eBook ISBN: 978-1-0879-4547-7

Cover and Formatting: Streetlight Graphics
Contact: johnmarinelli@embarqmail.com

This book is protected under US copyright laws. Any reproduction or other use is prohibited without the written permission of the author.

No part of this book may be reproduced, scanned, or distributed in any printed or electronic form without permission. Please do not participate in or encourage piracy of copyrighted materials in violation of the author's rights. Thank you for respecting the hard work of this author.

TABLE OF CONTENTS

Preface 1

Introduction 3

Chapter One: Schools of Thought 9

Chapter Two: Signs of The Times 21

Chapter Three: The Anti-Christ Revealed 34

Chapter Four: Our Waiting Posture & Perspectives 47

Chapter Five: False Christians & Religions 51

Chapter Six: What Some Folks Think About God 58

Chapter Seven: Resting In The Lord 61

Chapter Eight: What You Should Know 68

Chapter Nine: Being, "Born Again" Is Essential 74

Chapter Ten: Today's Manna From Heaven 78

Conclusion 87

About The Author John Marinelli 89

Gallery of Encouraging Christian Poems 90

PREFACE

The purpose of this book is to educate, inform and edify believers in Christ as to their divine destiny and encourage them to fight the good fight of faith until Jesus comes.

We will be discussing the why, when, how and aftermath of Jesus' return. We will look at some indicators that point to his 2nd coming.

We will discuss the concept of a "Rapture" and discuss the ideas of a pre-tribulation rapture opposed to a Mid, Post or No rapture at all.

We will examine the possibility of the Church going through the 7-year tribulation period spoken of in the books of Daniel and Revelation. We will also discuss who, if any, will be raptured and who will not.

We will list and discuss the signs of his (Jesus') coming and relate them to our day and times.

We will be using the King James version of the Bible to validate and support our premise and conclusions.

INTRODUCTION

I am sure you have heard that Jesus is planning to return to planet earth one day. When that day is, no one knows but God, the Father. Matthew 24:36 tells us, "But about that day or hour no one knows, not even the angels in heaven, nor the Son, but only the Father."

You'll remember that Jesus was given by God the father as an act of love to die for the sins of mankind. His mission was to defeat the devil and all evil forces and secure salvation for those who would believe.

"For God so loved the world, that he gave his only begotten Son, that whosoever believeth in him should not perish, but have everlasting life." John 3:16

John 3:16 is about **love** and the free gift of salvation to mankind. This scripture talks about the love that God has for his creation. It tells us that we are precious in the sight of God and worthy of redemption.

Jesus' purpose was to redeem mankind and re-establish the oneness that God and Adam had before his rebellion.

That being accomplished, he ascended into heaven to sit at the right hand of God, the father as our intercessor. "If ye then be risen with Christ, seek those things which are above, where Christ sits on the right hand of God." Colossians 3:1

The angels said, "Ye men of Galilee, why stand ye gazing up into heaven? This same Jesus, which is taken up from you into heaven, shall so come in like manner as ye have seen him go into heaven." Acts 1:11 Jesus made sure his followers knew why he was going away and that he would return.

"Let not your heart be troubled: ye believe in God, believe also in me. In my Father's house are many mansions: if it were not so, I would have told you. I go to prepare a place for you. And if I go and prepare a place for you, I will come again, and receive you unto myself; that where I am, there ye may be also. And whither I go ye know, and the way ye know.

Thomas saith unto him, Lord, we know not whither thou goest; and how can we know the way? Jesus saith unto him, **I am the Way, the Truth, and the Life: no man comes unto the Father, but by me.** John 14:1-6

It's been over 2,000 years since Jesus ascended into heaven to prepare a place for us. Some folks say he will never return. Others have predicted his return and were wrong. Here's a few to ponder:

- Three Christian theologians predicted Jesus would return in the year 500. One prediction was based on the dimensions of Noah's ark.
- A Spanish monk prophesied the second coming of Christ and the end of the world would take place that day to a crowd of people. That was 793.
- Believed that Jesus would return and the world would end this year. That was 1694.
- John Wesley, the founder of the Methodist Church, foresaw the Millennium beginning this year. He wrote that Revelation 12:14 referred to the years 1058–1836, "when Christ should come" That was 1836.
- George Rapp, the founder of the Harmony Society, preached that Jesus would return in his lifetime, even as he lay dying on 7 August 1847
- The first president of what is now the Watchtower Society of the Jehovah's Witnesses, calculated 1874 to be the year of Christ's Second Coming, and until his death taught that Christ was invisibly present, and ruling from the heavens from that date prophesied.
- The Catholic Apostle church, founded in 1831, claimed that Jesus would return by the time the last of its 12 founding members died. The last member died in 1901
- Herbert W. Armstrong, Pastor-General and self-proclaimed "Apostle"

of the Radio Church of God, and then the Worldwide Church of God, felt the return of Jesus Christ might be in 1975.
- Hal Lindsey published a book, "The Late Great Planet Earth," suggesting Christ would return in the 1980s, probably no later than 1988.
- Fundamentalist preacher Jerry Falwell predicted in 1999 that the Second Coming would probably be within 10 years.

End time events and the return of Jesus Christ are making headlines these days. But this is not new. Here are the top 7 Predictions on End Time Events and Return of Jesus.

1. Mark Biltz predicted the second coming of Christ to correspond with the September 28 (2015) lunar eclipse, a prediction known as Blood Moon Prophecy.

2. The Quran Code: The Quran Code is a numerology technique used to predict future, based on the belief that numbers often correlate to specific divine events. It purports that there's a hidden code in the Quran based on the number 19.

This preaching started in 1968 by Rashad Khalifa who claimed he had conversations with Archangel Gabriel. According to his computer analysis of the Quran's text, all of the names for God appeared in multiples of 19 times throughout the book.

For example, "Allah," which means god, (not the God of Abraham) appears in the Quran 2698 times, which is 19×142. Through this system, he was able to translate the entire hidden "code," and came to the conclusions that the end of the world will be in 2280 AD (19×120).

3. Jeane Dixon – 2020

The American self-proclaimed psychic and astrologer Jeane Dixon predicted Armageddon would take place in 2020 and Jesus would return to defeat the unholy Trinity of the Antichrist, Satan and the False Prophet between 2020 and 2037.

4. F. Kenton Beshore – 2021

Beshore already predicted Jesus would come back in 1988, i.e., within one Biblical generation (40 years) of the founding of Israel in 1948.

As his prediction failed to occur, he claims that the prediction was correct, but that the definition of a Biblical generation was incorrect and was actually 70–80 years.

In case you don't figure it out, he now predicts the Second Coming of Jesus between 2018 and 2028.

5. Kent Hovind – 2028

Kent E. Hovind is an American Young Earth Creationist, Christian fundamentalist, evangelist and tax protester.

In 2013, Hovind self-published a dissertation while in prison, to earn a Doctor of Ministry degree from the Patriot Bible University, in which he claims Jesus will return "During the feast of Trumpets in 2028."

6. Mike Flipp (Sign of Two) – 2029

Over a period of two years, 2004 to 2005, Mr. Mike Flipp claimed to see signs that were related to the number 2.

According to his website and book called 2!, "These signs lead to the manifestation of a "Cross" formed perfectly over the United States in which there is something that the Lord is going to do at 9 points along the shape of a cross over the United States, and there are signs which lead to the 2nd coming of Jesus Christ"

Decoding these signs, allowed him to find that the second coming of Christ would occur in 2029.

7. Frank J. Tipler – By 2057

In 2007, Mr. Tipler published a sequel on the physics of immortality", called "The Physics of Christianity", in which he predicted the Second Coming of Christ to occur within 50 years, that is by 2057.

He also claimed the event will be coincident with Singularity, which futurist Ray Kurzweil has predicted will occur by 2045.

Predictions, as you can see, have been made over the centuries but have not come true. Remember, only the Father knows when it will happen.

CHAPTER ONE:
SCHOOLS OF THOUGHT

I think that we can all agree that Jesus will return to earth sometime in the future. It could be as you are reading this book or many years from now. Trying to figure out when is pointless. What may be more interesting is positioning the event in relationship to the 7-year tribulation period mentioned in the books of Daniel and Revelation. There are three schools of thought... Pre-Trib, Mid-Trib and Post-Trib.

The 7-year time period mentioned is also known as...

- The great tribulation (Matthew 24:21)
- The Day of the Lord (Isaiah 2:12; 13:6-9; Joel 1:15; 2:1-31; 3:14; 1 Thessalonians 5:2)
- Trouble or tribulation (Deuteronomy 4:30)
- The time of Jacob's troubles (Jeremiah 30:7)

There are some things to know about the "Great Tribulation."

- **Seven angels will pour out God's wrath upon the earth.**

"Then I heard a loud voice from the temple saying to the seven angels, 'Go and pour out the bowls of the wrath of God on the earth.'"–Revelation 16:1

- **God's wrath will be worse than anything in history.**

"For then there will be great tribulation, such as has not been since the beginning of the world until this time, no, nor ever shall be."–Matthew 24:21

- **The Church will not experience the wrath of God.**

"For the Lord Himself will descend from heaven with a shout, with the voice of an archangel, and with the trumpet of God. And the dead in Christ will rise first. Then we who are alive and remain shall be caught up together with them in the clouds to meet the Lord in the air. And thus, we shall always be with the Lord. Therefore comfort one another with these words."–1 Thessalonians 4:15-18

"For God did not appoint us to wrath, but to obtain salvation through our Lord Jesus Christ." 1 Thessalonians 5:9

Author's Note: I believe that there are two separate events that take place. Both relate to the 2nd coming. The 1st is the rapture of the church where Jesus comes for his church which are all, "Born Again," believers as well as those that died in the Lord. They are taken up to be with him. This is shown in the above scripture. The actual 2nd coming is when Jesus descends from heaven and the tribes of the earth will see him and mourn. Matthew 24:29-30 The rapture is part of the 2nd coming but Jesus does not stay. He leaves with his church and returns after the tribulation to fight the final battle between good and evil and to judge those who are left.

- **It will involve the safety of Israel.**

"Alas! For the day is great, so that none is like it; and it is the time of Jacob's [Israel's] trouble, but he shall be saved out of it."–Jeremiah 30:7

- **Many will be saved during this time.**

"'Who are these arrayed in white robes, and where did they come from?'… So he said to me, 'These are the ones who came out of the great tribulation, and washed their robes and made them white in the blood of the Lamb."–Revelation 7:13,14

The 7-year tribulation will be beyond anything we can imagine. The trouble the earth sees will be unlike any other trouble that human history has ever known. Jesus said this in Matthew 24:21…

- "For then there will be great tribulation, such as has not been since the beginning of the world until this time, no, nor ever shall be."

To put it mildly, it's going to get bad.

The Old Testament prophet Daniel said, "that it shall be times, times, and a half; and when the power of the holy people has been completely shattered, all these things shall be finished." "Times, time, and half a time" is three and a half years. This is the halfway point through the 7-year tribulation.

Jesus said, "Therefore when you see the 'abomination of desolation,' spoken of by Daniel the prophet, standing in the holy place…" This abomination of desolation warns us about the beast putting up an image in the temple that he makes the world worship.

Daniel 9:27 said this would happen in the middle of a "week," which is 7 years. Revelation 11:2, 13:5, and Daniel 12:11 noted that the beast would do this for 42 months.

The first three and a half years will be a time of false peace and prosperity upon the earth, as the Anti-Christ will make a treaty with the people of Israel. At the halfway point, the beast will set up an image in the temple, desecrating it. This begins the second half of the 7-year tribulation, and then God's wrath is poured out until his judgment is completed.

It is Christ himself who used the phrase "*Great Tribulation*" with reference to the last half of the Tribulation. In Matthew 24:21, Jesus says,

"For then there will be a great tribulation, such as has not occurred since the beginning of the world until now, nor ever shall." In this verse Jesus is referring to the event of Matthew 24:15, which describes the revealing of the abomination of desolation, the man also known as the Anti-Christ.

Also, Jesus, in Matthew 24:29-30 states, "Immediately after the tribulation of those days . . . the Son of Man will appear in the sky, and then all the tribes of the earth will mourn, and they will see the Son of Man coming on the clouds of the sky with power and great glory."

In this passage, Jesus defines the Great Tribulation (v.21) as beginning with the revealing of the abomination of desolation (v.15) and ending with Christ's second coming (v.30).

Another passage that refers to the Great Tribulation is Daniel 12:1b, which says, "And there will be a time of distress such as never occurred since there was a nation until that time."

It seems that Jesus was quoting this verse when he spoke the words recorded in Matthew 24:21. Also referring to the Great Tribulation is Jeremiah 30:7,

"Alas! for that day is great, there is none like it; And it is the time of Jacob's distress, but he will be saved from it." The phrase "Jacob's distress" refers to the nation of Israel, which will experience persecution and natural disasters such as have never before been seen.

Considering the information Christ gave us in Matthew 24:15-30, it is easy to conclude that the beginning of the Great Tribulation has much to do with the abomination of desolation, an action of the Anti-Christ.

In Daniel 9:26-27, we find that this man will make a "covenant" (a peace pact) with the world for seven years.

Halfway through the seven-year period—"in the middle of the week"—we are told this man will break the covenant he made, stopping sacrifice and grain offering, which specifically refers to his actions in the rebuilt temple of the future.

Revelation 13:1-10 gives even more detail concerning the Beast's actions, and just as important, it also verifies the length of time he will be in power. Revelation 13:5 says he will be in power for 42 months, which is three and one-half years, the length of the Great Tribulation.

Revelation offers us the most information about the Great Tribulation. From Revelation 13 when the "Beast" is revealed until Christ returns in Revelation 19, we are given a picture of God's wrath on the earth because of unbelief and rebellion. (Excerpts from GotQuestions.com)

The Pre-Tribulation folks see the 2nd coming as the rapture of the church.

It's been said that Jesus will come for his church on earth and rapture it into his presence. It is a catching away of all Christians, real ones, not religious fakes or even churchgoers that play church for other selfish reasons.

The word rapture (in Greek harpazo, in Latin rapere) means to be caught up or taken away suddenly. The rapture refers to the sudden removal of all of God's people on the earth. In the twinkling of an eye, "Born Again" Christians will suddenly be transformed and will rise up into the air to join Jesus Christ.

There is a reason Christ warned his followers 13 times in the New Testament to not be deceived, and to watch and be ready. He wanted us to be excited about his glorious appearing.

Satan, on the other hand, does not want us to be excited. He is the master deceiver; the father of lies and wants us to believe his deception rather than the signs of Christ's return given to us by Jesus himself. He will send many lies to deceive us and to rob us of the joy of living every day in anticipation of Christ's return.

For those who believe that the Bible is the truth and is the very Word of God, it's easy to believe in and rejoice in the prophecies that tell of the rapture of God's church. The Bible tells us of others who have been taken up into heaven in very much the same way that we will be at the time of the rapture.

Elijah was taken up into heaven like a whirlwind. I Kings 2:11-12 "As they were walking along and talking together, suddenly a chariot of fire and horses of fire appeared and separated the two of them, and Elijah went up to heaven in a whirlwind. Elisha saw this and cried out, "My father! My father! The chariots and horsemen of Israel! And Elisha saw him no more."

Enoch was also taken from this life so that he would not experience death. Hebrews 11:5 "By faith Enoch was taken from this life, so that he did not experience death; he could not be found, because God had taken him away. for before he was taken, he was commended as one who pleased God, and without faith it is impossible to please God, because anyone who comes to him must believe that he exists and that he rewards those who earnestly seek him."

So, when will the church be raptured? We know there is more evidence today that he is coming for his church soon, than at any other time in history. As these signs intensify, all of us who know Christ as our savior will be looking toward heaven and awaiting the coming of our Lord.

Many Biblical scholars feel that the rapture will occur prior to the "Tribulation Period", or a pre-tribulation rapture. Thus, God will spare his church from the persecutions of the Anti-Christ and the wrath of God that will fall upon the inhabitants of the earth during the end times.

Those who come to Christ following the rapture will live through the persecution of Christians by the Anti-Christ. Some will face martyrdom for their faith.

There are several other views of the timing for the rapture of the church; however, first we will examine the pre-tribulation view and the Biblical support for it.

Best supporting verse… One of the best supporting verses from the Bible for the rapture of the church is found in Revelation 3:10.

"Because you have kept my command to persevere, I also will keep you from the hour of trial which shall come upon the whole world to test those who dwell on the earth."

I would assume that God would not bring the same type of judgment to his children, as he will on the wicked. This scripture seems to support my premise. The assumption is that Believers will be taken out of harm's way.

Listen to what Paul tells the Thessalonians in his second letter, chapter two verses 2-15.

"Now we beseech you, brethren, by the coming of our Lord Jesus Christ, and by our gathering together unto him, that ye be not soon shaken in mind, or be troubled, neither by spirit, nor by word, nor by letter as from us, as that the day of Christ is at hand.

Let no man deceive you by any means: for that day shall not come, except there come a falling away first, and that man of sin be revealed, the son of perdition; who opposes and exalts himself above all that is called God, or that is worshipped; so that he, as God, sits in the temple of God, shewing himself that he is God.

Remember ye not, that, when I was yet with you, I told you these things? And now ye know what withholds that he might be revealed in his time. For the mystery of iniquity doth already work: only he who now letteth will let**,** until he be taken out of the way.

And then shall that wicked be revealed, whom the Lord shall consume with the spirit of his mouth, and shall destroy with the brightness of his coming: even him, whose coming is after the working of Satan with all power and signs and lying wonders, and with all deceivableness of unrighteousness in them that perish; because they received not the love of the truth that they might be saved.

And for this cause God shall send them strong delusion, that they should believe a lie: that they all might be damned who believed not the truth, but had pleasure in unrighteousness.

But we are bound to give thanks always to God for you, brethren, beloved of the Lord, because God hath from the beginning chosen you to salvation through sanctification of the Spirit and belief of the truth: whereunto he called you by our gospel, to the obtaining of the glory of our Lord Jesus Christ.

Therefore, brethren, stand fast, and hold the traditions, which ye have been taught, whether by word, or our epistle."

I wanted to show the context so there is no misunderstanding. Note verse seven…he that letteth (Meaning Restrains) is God's Holy Spirit. He is the restraining force in the world, holding evil back from its ultimate expression.

You may want to know how the Holy Spirit restrains evil from expressing itself. "And when he has come, he will convict the world of sin, and of righteousness, and of judgment: of sin, because they do not believe in me; of righteousness, because I go to my Father and you see me no more; of judgment, because the ruler of this world is judged." John 6:8-11

When the Spirit is taken out of the way, there is no more conviction of sin. Guess what? the Spirit is in us and Jesus said he would never leave us comfortless but will be with us until the end of the age. (John 14:18) When that moment has come, it will be the end of the age and we will go with the Spirit to meet Jesus in the air as Paul says in 1 Thessalonians 4:17.

Judgment cannot happen until the Holy Spirit is taken out of the way, and then shall that wicked one be revealed. (The Anti-Christ) This is a pre-tribulation departure.

There are others that hold to a Mid-Tribulation departure of the church. The thought is that the first 3 ½ years are not so bad. However, the Anti-Christ being revealed kicks off the tribulation. That's when the clock starts ticking. The full 7-years are considered the pouring out of God's wrath.

1 Thessalonians 5:9 tell us that the church will not experience God's wrath. This is because the church has been made righteous by grace through faith in the completed work of Jesus Christ on the Cross.

God never pours out wrath on the righteous. Behold, the whirlwind of the LORD goes forth with fury, a continuing whirlwind: it shall fall with pain upon the head of the wicked. Jeramiah 30:23

In summary, the mid-tribulation rapture is not sound Biblical doctrine. The only view that is sound and takes in consideration of the entire "big picture" of Bible prophecy is the pre-tribulation rapture.

Finally, there are those that feel that Jesus will return at the end of the 7-year tribulation period.

When considering any question involving eschatology (the study of end times), it is important to remember that almost all Christians agree on these three things:

1) There is coming a time of great tribulation such as the world has never seen,

2) After the Tribulation, Christ will return to establish his kingdom on earth,

3) There will be a Rapture—a "catching away" from mortality to immortality—for believers as described in John 14:1-3, 1 Corinthians 15:51-52, and 1 Thessalonians 4:16-17. The only question regards the timing of the Rapture: when will it occur in relation to the Tribulation and the Second Coming?

Post-tribulation proponents teach that the Rapture occurs at the end, or near the end, of the Tribulation. At that time, the church will meet Christ in the air and then return to earth for the commencement of Christ's Kingdom on earth.

In other words, the Rapture and Christ's Second Coming (to set up his Kingdom) happen almost simultaneously. According to this view, the church goes through the entire seven-year Tribulation. Roman Catholicism, Greek Orthodoxy, and many Protestant denominations espouse a post-tribulation view.

One weakness of post-tribulation view is the clear teaching of Scripture that those who are in Christ are not under condemnation and will never experience the wrath of God (Romans 8:1). While some judgments during the Tribulation specifically target the unsaved, many other judgments, such as the earthquakes, falling stars, and famines, will affect the saved and unsaved equally. Thus, if believers go through the Tribulation, they will experience the wrath of God, in contradiction of Romans 8:1.

The Post-tribulation view also face a difficulty in explaining the absence of the word church in all Biblical passages related to the tribulation. Even in Revelation 4: 21, the lengthiest description of the tribulation in all of Scripture, the word church never appears. Post-tribulation folks must assume that the word saints in Revelation 4: 21 means the church, although a different Greek word is used.

And a final weakness of the post-tribulation view is shared by the other two theories: namely, the Bible does not give an explicit time line concerning future events. Scripture does not expressly teach one view over another, and that is why we have diversity of opinion concerning the end times and some variety on how the related prophecies should be harmonized. (Excerpts from GotQuestions.com)

Author's Note: It is my opinion that the pre-tribulation is the most accurate interpretation. That is why I support it.

Scriptures Relating To The Rapture of The Church And The 2nd Coming of Christ

1 Thessalonians 4:17 - Then we which are alive and remain shall be caught up together with them in the clouds, to meet the Lord in the air: and so shall we ever be with the Lord.

Luke 17:34-37 - I tell you, in that night there shall be two men in one bed; the one shall be taken, and the other shall be left.

1 Thessalonians 4:16 - For the Lord himself shall descend from heaven with a shout, with the voice of the archangel, and with the trump of God: and the dead in Christ shall rise first:

Revelation 3:10 - Because thou hast kept the word of my patience, I also will keep thee from the hour of temptation, which shall come upon all the world, to try them that dwell upon the earth.

Mark 13:32 - But of that day and that hour knows no man, no, not the angels which are in heaven, neither the Son, but the Father.

Matthew 24:29-31 - Immediately after the tribulation of those days shall the sun be darkened, and the moon shall not give her light, and the stars shall fall from heaven, and the powers of the heavens shall be shaken:

1 Corinthians 15:52 - In a moment, in the twinkling of an eye, at the last trump: for the trumpet shall sound, and the dead shall be raised incorruptible, and we shall be changed.

Daniel 12:1-2 - And at that time shall Michael stand up, the great prince which stands for the children of thy people: and there shall be a time of trouble, such as never was since there was a nation even to that same time: and at that time thy people shall be delivered, every one that shall be found written in the book.

1 Thessalonians 5:9 - For God hath not appointed us to wrath, but to obtain salvation by our Lord Jesus Christ.

Matthew 24:31 - And he shall send his angels with a great sound of a trumpet, and they shall gather together his elect from the four winds, from one end of heaven to the other.

Luke 12:40 - Be ye therefore ready also: for the Son of man cometh at an hour when ye think not.

Romans 10:9 - That if thou shalt confess with thy mouth the Lord Jesus, and shalt believe in thine heart that God hath raised him from the dead, thou shalt be saved.

Revelation 20:2-5 - And he laid hold on the dragon, that old serpent, which is the Devil, and Satan, and bound him a thousand years.

1 Thessalonians 5:2 - For yourselves know perfectly that the day of the Lord so cometh as a thief in the night.

Matthew 24:42 - Watch therefore: for ye know not what hour your Lord doth come.

Luke 17:34 - I tell you, in that night there shall be two men in one bed; the one shall be taken, and the other shall be left.

2 Thessalonians 2:3-7 - Let no man deceive you by any means: for that day shall not come, except there come a falling away first, and that man of sin be revealed, the son of perdition;

Mark 13:32-37 - But of that day and that hour knows no man, no, not the angels which are in heaven, neither the Son, but the Father.

Matthew 24:27 - For as the lightning cometh out of the east, and shineth even unto the west; so shall also the coming of the Son of man be.

CHAPTER TWO:
SIGNS OF THE TIMES

Now as he sat on the Mount of Olives, the disciples came to him privately, saying, "tell us, when will these things be? And what will be the sign of your coming, and of the end of the age?"

And Jesus answered and said to them: "Take heed that no one *deceives you*. For many will come in my name, saying, 'I am the Christ,' and will deceive many. And you will hear of wars and rumors of wars. See that you are not troubled; for all these things must come to pass, but the end is not yet. For nation will rise against nation, and kingdom against kingdom. And there will be famines, pestilences, and earthquakes in various places. All these are the beginning of sorrows.

Then they will deliver you up to tribulation and kill you, and you will be hated by all nations for my name's sake. And then many will be offended, will betray one another, and will hate one another. Then many false prophets will rise up and deceive many. And because lawlessness will abound, the love of many will grow cold. But he who endures to the end shall be saved. And this gospel of the kingdom will be preached in all the world as a witness to all the nations, and then the end will come." Matthew 24:3-14

These are the signs of the times before the end of time which also relates to the 2nd coming of Jesus:

1. Attempts to deceive believers.

    Jesus knew that there would be those that will try to deceive his disciples. He specifically said that they should, "Take Heed" In other words, pay particular attention to folks with different beliefs and be sure to know all that Jesus told them so they do not go astray. Then he begins to tell them why.

2. Many false Christs will come saying they are Jesus. Take a look at this list of false Christ that rose up over the past:

Men Who Claimed To Be The Christ

18TH CENTURY

- Kondratiy Selivanov (1730s-1842) - Founder of the Skoptsy sect
- Ann Lee (1736-1784) - Founder of "The Shakers"

19TH CENTURY

John Nichols Thom (1799–1838), a tax rebel who claimed to be the "savior of the world" and the reincarnation of Jesus Christ in 1834. He was killed by British soldiers at the Battle of Bossenden Wood, on May 31, 1838 in Kent, England.

- Arnold Potter (1804–1872), Schismatic "Latter Day Saints" leader; he claimed the spirit of Jesus Christ entered into his body and he became "Potter Christ" Son of the living God. He died in an attempt to ascend to heaven by jumping off a cliff. His body was later retrieved and buried by his followers.
- Jones Very (1813–1880), American essayist, poet, literary scholar, and Greek tutor at Harvard who befriended several prominent American Transcendentalists and suffered a nervous breakdown in 1837 after which he claimed to have become the Second Coming of Jesus.
- Baháʼuʼlláh (1817–1892), born Shiite, adopted Bábism later in 1844, he claimed to be the prophesied fulfillment and Promised

One of three major religions. He founded the Bahá'í Faith in 1863. Followers of the Bahá'í Faith believe that the fulfillment of the prophecies of the second coming of Jesus, as well as the prophecies of the 5th Buddha Maitreya and many other religious prophecies, were begun by the Báb in 1844 and then by Bahá'u'lláh. They commonly compare the fulfillment of Christian prophecies to Jesus' fulfillment of Jewish prophecies.

- William W. Davies (1833–1906), leader of a "Latter Day Saint" schismatic group called the Kingdom of Heaven located in Walla Walla, Washington from 1867 to 1881. He taught his followers that he was the archangel Michael, who had previously lived as the biblical Adam, Abraham, and David. When his son Arthur was born on February 11, 1868, Davies declared that the infant was the reincarnated Jesus Christ. When Davies's second son, David, was born in 1869, he was declared to be God the Father.

- Mirza Ghulam Ahmad of Qadian, India (1835–1908), claimed to be the awaited Mahdi as well and likeness of Jesus, the promised Messiah at the end of time. He claimed to be Jesus in the metaphorical sense; in character. He founded the Ahmadiyya Movement in 1889, envisioning it to be the rejuvenation of Islam, and claimed to be commissioned by God for the reformation of mankind.

20TH CENTURY

- John Hugh Smyth-Pigott (1852–1927). Around 1890 Smyth-Pigott started leading meetings of the Agapenomite community and recruited 50 young female followers to supplement its ageing population. He took Ruth Anne Preece as his second wife and she had three children named Glory, Power and Hallelujah. By 1902 his fame had spread as far as India, from where Mirza Ghulam Ahmad warned him of his false teachings and predicted his miserable end. Smyth-Pigott died in 1927 and the sect gradually declined until the last member, sister Ruth, died in 1956. Her funeral in 1956 was the only time when outsiders were admitted to the chapel.

- Haile Selassie I (1892–1975). While Selsassie did not claim to be Jesus and disapproved of claims that he was Jesus, the Rastafari movement, which emerged in Jamaica during the 1930s, believes he is the Second Coming. He embodied this when he became Emperor of Ethiopia in 1930, perceived as confirmation of the return of the Messiah in the prophetic Book of Revelation 5:5 in the New Testament, who is also expected to return a second time to initiate the apocalyptic day of judgment. He is also called Jah Ras Tafari, and is often considered to be alive by Rastafari movement members.
- Lou de Palingboer (1898–1968), the founder and figurehead of a new religious movement in the Netherlands, who claimed to be "the resurrected body of Jesus Christ".
- Ernest Norman (1904–1971), an American electrical engineer who co-founded the Unarius Academy of Science in 1954, was allegedly Jesus in a past life and his earthly incarnation was as an archangel named Raphael. He claimed to be the reincarnation of other notable figures including Confucius, Mona Lisa, Benjamin Franklin, Socrates, Queen Elizabeth I, and Tsar Peter I the Great.
- Krishna Venta (1911–1958), born Francis Herman Pencovic in San Francisco, founded the WKFL (Wisdom, Knowledge, Faith and Love) Fountain of the World cult in Simi Valley, California in the late 1940s. In 1948 he stated that he was Christ, the new messiah and claimed to have led a convoy of rocket ships to Earth from the extinct planet Neophrates. He died on December 10, 1958 after being suicide bombed by two disgruntled former followers who accused Venta of mishandling cult funds and having been intimate with their wives.
- Ahn Sahng-Hong (1918–1985), a South Korean who founded the World Mission Society Church of God in 1964, who recognize him as the Second Coming of Jesus. The World Mission Society Church of God teach that Zahng Gil-jah is "God the Mother", who they explain is referred to in the Bible as the New Jerusalem Mother (Galatians4:26), and that Ahn Sahng-Hong is God the Father.
- Sun Myung Moon (1920–2012), believed by members of the Unification Church to be the Messiah and the Second Coming of Christ, fulfilling Jesus' unfinished mission. Church members

("Unificationists") consider Sun Myung Moon and his wife, Hak Ja Han, to be the True Parents of humankind as the restored Adam and Eve.

- Jim Jones (1931–1978), founder of Peoples Temple, which started off as an offshoot of a mainstream Protestant sect before becoming a personality cult as time went on. He claimed to be the reincarnation of Jesus, Akhenaten, the Buddha, Vladimir Lenin, and Father Divine in the 1970s. He organized a mass murder suicide at Jonestown, Guyana on November 18, 1978. He shot himself after the murders were done.
- Marshall Applewhite (1931–1997), an American who posted a Usenet message declaring, "I, Jesus—Son of God—acknowledge on this date of September 25/26, 1995: ..." Applewhite and his Heaven's Gate religious group committed mass suicide on March 26, 1997 to rendezvous with what they thought was a spaceship hiding behind Comet Hale–Bopp.
- Yahweh ben Yahweh (1935–2007), born as Hulon Mitchell, Jr., a black nationalist and separatist who created the Nation of Yahweh in 1979 in Liberty City, Florida. His self-proclaimed name means "God, Son of God". He could have only been deeming himself to be "son of God", not God, but many of his followers clearly deem him to be God Incarnate. In 1992, he was convicted of conspiracy to commit murder and sentenced to 18 years in prison.
- Laszlo Toth (1938–2012), Hungarian-born Australian who claimed he was Jesus Christ as he vandalized Michelangelo's Pietà with a geologist's hammer in 1972.
- Wayne Bent (1941–), also known as Michael Travesser of the Lord Our Righteousness Church. He claims: "I am the embodiment of God. I am divinity and humanity combined." He was convicted on December 15, 2008 of one count of criminal sexual contact of a minor and two counts of contributing to the delinquency of a minor in 2008.
- Ariffin Mohammed (1943–2016), also known as "Ayah Pin", the founder of the banned Sky Kingdom in Malaysia in 1975. He claimed to have direct contact with the heavens and is believed by his

followers to have been the incarnation of Jesus, as well as Shiva, and the Buddha, and Muhammad.

- Mitsuo Matayoshi (1944–), a conservative Japanese politician, who in 1997 established the World Economic Community Party based on his conviction that he is God and Christ, renaming himself Iesu Matayoshi. According to his program he will do the Last Judgment as Christ but within the current political system.
- José Luis de Jesús Miranda (1946–2013), Puerto Rican founder, leader and organizer of Growing in Grace based in Miami, Florida, who claimed that the resurrected Christ "integrated himself within me" in 2007.
- Inri Cristo (1948–), a Brazilian who claims to be the second Jesus reincarnated in 1969, Brasília is considered by Inri Cristo and his disciples as the New Jerusalem of the Apocalypse.
- Thomas Harrison Provenzano (1949–2000), an American convicted murderer who was possibly mentally ill. He compared his execution with Jesus Christ's crucifixion.
- Shoko Asahara (1955–), founded the controversial Japanese religious group Aum Shinrikyo in 1984. He declared himself Christ, Japan's only fully enlightened master and the Lamb of God. His purported mission was to take upon himself the sins of the world. He outlined a doomsday prophecy, which included a Third World War, and described a final conflict culminating in a nuclear Armageddon. Humanity would end, except for the elite few who joined Aum. The group gained international notoriety on March 20, 1995, when it carried out the Sarin gas attack on the Tokyo subway. He has been sentenced to death, and is awaiting execution.
- David Koresh (1959–1993), born Vernon Wayne Howell, was the leader of a Branch Davidian religious sect in Waco, Texas, though never directly claiming to be Jesus himself, proclaimed that he was the final prophet and "the Son of God, the Lamb" in 1983. In 1993, a raid by the U.S. BATF, and the subsequent siege by the FBI ended with Branch Davidian ranch burning to the ground. Koresh, 54 adults and 21 children were found dead after the fire extinguished itself.

- Hogen Fukunaga (1945–) founded Ho No Hana Sanpogyo, often called the "foot reading cult", in Japan in 1987 after an alleged spiritual event where he claimed to have realized he was the reincarnation of Jesus Christ and Gautama Buddha.
- Marina Tsvigun (1960–), or Maria Devi Christos, is the leader of the Great White Brotherhood. In 1990 she met Yuri Krivonogov, the Great White Brotherhood founder, who recognized Marina as a new messiah and later married her, assuming in the sect the role of John the Baptist, subordinate to Tsvigun.
- Sergey Torop (1961–), a Russian who claims to be "reborn" as Vissarion, Jesus Christ returned, which makes him not "God" but the "Word of God". Also known as "Jesus of Siberia," Torop has an appearance similar to depictions of Jesus. He dresses in all white flowing robes and has long brown hair and a beard.

Before claiming to be the Vissarion, Torop worked as a traffic policeman until he was fired in 1990. He founded the Church of the Last Testament and the spiritual community Ecopolis Tiberkul in Southern Siberia in 1990. The Church of the Last Testament has been described as being a mixture of beliefs from the Russian Orthodox Church, Buddhism, apocalypticism, collectivism, and with ecological values. The church currently resides on the largest religious reservation in the world in Siberian Taiga.

21ST CENTURY

Apollo Quiboloy (1950–) is the founder and leader of a Philippines-based Restorationist church, the Kingdom of Jesus Christ, The Name Above Every Name, Inc. He has made claims that he is the "Appointed Son of God".

Alan John Miller (1962–), more commonly known as A.J. Miller, a former Jehovah's Witness elder and current leader of the Australia-based Divine Truth movement. Miller claims to be Jesus Christ reincarnated with others in the 20th century to spread messages that he calls the "Divine Truth". He delivers these messages in seminars and various forms of media along with his current partner Mary Suzanne Luck, who identifies herself as the returned Mary Magdalene.

David Shayler (1965–) is a former MI5 agent and whistleblower who, in the summer of 2007, proclaimed himself to be the Messiah. He has released a series of videos on YouTube claiming to be Jesus, although he has not built up any noticeable following since his claims.

Maurice Clemmons (1972–2009) an American felon responsible for the 2009 murder of four police officers in Washington state, referred to himself in May 2009 as Jesus.

Oscar Ramiro Ortega-Hernandez (1990–). In November 2011, he fired nine shots with a Romanian Cugir SA semi-automatic rifle at the White House in Washington D.C., believing himself to be Jesus Christ sent to kill U.S. President Barack Obama, whom he believed to be the antichrist.

3. Wars and rumors of wars.

This statement of wars and rumors of wars is not really a sign of the end times or the return of Jesus. If we read on, we will hear that Jesus says we should not be concerned because the end is not yet. He just wanted his followers to know that it was not to be looked at as a sign but rather a series of events that will happen all the time.

4. Famines, pestilences, and earthquakes in various places.

Weather activity like earthquakes, famine and pestilence are also natural happenings as the creation groans being in turmoil. I see this as a marker on the way to the main event.

5. You will be hated by all nations for my name's sake.

Being hated is a reference 1st of all to the nation of Israel. The Jews have been hated by most all nations, even the United States many times in the past. Finally, the warning also applies to Christians that walk in the Spirit to do the Will of God. They too are hated because those who hate them are controlled by evil forces. The hate comes mainly because we are followers of Jesus. It is for his name's sake that we suffer persecution.

6. Many will be offended, will betray one another, and will hate one another.

Betrayal comes when jealousy rules the day. There are times when we are just doing our own thing and it bothers those around us. We could sing better or look prettier or drive a better car or almost anything and we will run into 2-faced brethren that will betray our confidence. It is always best to hold everybody at arm's length until they prove to your satisfaction that they can be trusted.

7. Many false prophets will rise up.

A false prophet is no more than an anti-Christ. They seek to deceive, manipulate and control everyone that will listen. They claim to be anointed of God but are really wolves in sheep's clothing.

Spotting a false prophet is easy. They will not accept the truth of the gospel, especially the doctrine of Incarnation (Christ In You and God being manifested in Jesus.) John 1:14 says that the Word became flesh and dwelt among us. This is God in man. They also reject the Deity of Jesus and reject his pre-existence as God before the foundation of the world.

8. Lawlessness will abound, the love of many will grow cold.

Have you seen folks running around in rebellion against the laws off our country? I have. They hate any law that restrains evil activity. The recent defunding off the police is a good example.

When love waxes cold, lawlessness abounds and can destroy a city, state or even a family. However, all of this is still road signs along the way to the end.

9. And this gospel of the kingdom will be preached in all the world as a witness to all the nations.

This gospel of the Kingdom has already been preached in all the world. This is a valid sign that must happen before the return of Jesus. The gospel message that Jesus was sent by God to save all that will believe has been accomplished in every nation.

Here are a few more signs:

10. People living without regard to God. Genesis 6:5, Luke 17:26-7

That is all around us. It was sparked by evolution and is commonplace today.

11. Explosion of knowledge and travel - Daniel - 12:4

Cars, trains, airplanes and space ships all testify to folks traveling more now than ever before. I have heard that knowledge doubles every 5-years. By the time we buy an electronic device, it is old hat. New stuff is on its way.

12. Widespread acceptance of immoral behavior - Luke 17:26, 2 Peter 2:5-8

How about sex trafficking, abuse, free love, prostitution, gay rights, transvestites, bi-sexually, movies that promote immorality and let's not forget pornography. They are seeking to change the very fabric of our society and moral compass.

13. Instability in world leadership - Psalm 2:1-3, Revelation 13:4-9

This is happening right now as I pen this text. The United States government is a joke and has created worldwide instability in the global economy. It's all due to poor choices and weak leadership. But we are not alone. Other nations are floundering as well.

14. The rebirth of the nation of Israel.

The scriptures tell us that the fig tree is a major sign. Matthew 24:32 indicates that when you see leaves on the fig tree you know that spring is coming soon. In the same way, you see the signs and you know and expect something to happen soon after. That something is the 2nd coming of Jesus. Matthew 24:3

These are linked to the 2nd coming when Jesus comes to earth to judge its inhabitants, not the rapture.

"Fearful sights and great signs shall there be from heaven, and there shall be signs in the sun and in the moon and in the stars; and upon the earth distress of nations, with perplexity; the sea and the waves roaring; men's hearts failing them for fear, and for looking after those things which are coming on the earth: for the powers of heaven shall be shaken." (Luke 21 v.10-11, 25-26)

Read more: https://www.whatchristianswanttoknow.com/biblical-signs-of-the-second-coming-of-jesus-christ/#ixzz7shROTiyg

Paul tells us about end times and signs to look for. He says;

"This know also, that in the last days perilous times shall come. For men shall be lovers of their own selves, covetous, boasters, proud, blasphemers, disobedient to parents, unthankful, unholy, without natural affection, trucebreakers, false accusers, incontinent, fierce, despisers of those that are good, traitors, heady, high-minded, lovers of pleasures more than lovers of God; Having a form of godliness, but denying the power thereof: from such turn away.

For of this sort are they which creep into houses, and lead captive silly women laden with sins, led away with divers lusts, Ever learning, and never able to come to the knowledge of the truth." (2 Timothy 3:1-7)

According to this, a communication gap is not the problem. The cause of increasing immorality is simply an increase in pride and sinfulness.

Read more: https://www.whatchristianswanttoknow.com/biblical-signs-of-the-second-coming-of-jesus-christ/#ixzz7shTtyTxR

The apostle Paul accurately predicted, "The time will come when men will not put up with sound doctrine. Instead, to suit their own desires, they will gather around them a great number of teachers to say what their itching ears want to hear. They will turn their ears away from the truth and turn aside to myths" (2 Tim. 4:3, 4). It is understood, the "desires" which some will try to "suit" are sinful! Could it be that doctrinal mythology is the result of people with "itching ears" turning to "a great number of teachers" who will say what itching ears with sinful desires want to hear?

Without Natural Affection – One of the most basic Judeo-Christian principles has been the natural and beautiful attraction between the sexes. The love of a mother and father for their children, the love of the extended family for each other, and the love of one's country were similarly considered "natural."

Today we are living in a depraved, Romans chapter one, world that many fear God has given or will give up to "vile passions" that reverse the normal order of things. (Roman 1 v.26-27)

Read more: https://www.whatchristianswanttoknow.com/biblical-signs-of-the-second-coming-of-jesus-christ/#ixzz7shWL0YSq

It is fascinating to note that almost 2000 years ago the apostle Peter, an untrained Galilean fisherman, predicted the exact thinking patterns that would characterize these scoffers.

He prophesied that ... "Scoffers will come in the last days, walking according to their own lusts, and saying, "Where is the promise of his coming? For since the fathers fell asleep, all things continue as they were from the beginning of creation."

For this they willfully forget: that by the word of God the heavens were of old, and the earth standing out of water and in the water, by which the world that then existed perished, being flooded with water. But the heavens and the earth which now exist are kept in store by the same word, reserved for fire until the Day of Judgment and perdition of ungodly men." (2 Peter 3 v.3-7)

Why does Peter say that the scoffers are so blind? He provides us with 2 reasons why: The first is found in 2 Peter 3 v5, "For this they willfully forget."

The unregenerate minds of unbelievers resist the idea of the intervention of God in human affairs. Their problem is spiritual, a matter of the will, and the unbeliever remains deliberately ignorant of the truth. Peter mentions a second reason for the scoffer's intellectual blindness in verse 3. He was told that "the words are closed up and sealed till the time of the end."

Read more:

https://www.whatchristianswanttoknow.com/
biblical-signs-of-the-second-coming-of-jesus-christ/#ixzz7shXPoYS8

CHAPTER THREE:
THE ANTI-CHRIST REVEALED

THE ANTICHRIST… In some Christian teachings, a personal opponent of Christ expected to appear before the end of the world: *"the battle between Christ and the Antichrist"* The term, "Anti-Christ" is defined as:

- a person or force seen as opposing Christ or the Christian Church:
- *"St. Paul really did have to fear for his life at the hands of an Antichrist named Nero"*
- a person or thing regarded as supremely evil or as a fundamental enemy or opponent:

Robert Lerner of Britannica tells us that the Christian conception of Antichrist was derived from Jewish traditions, particularly The Book of Daniel in the Hebrew Bible. Written about 167 BCE, it foretold the coming of a final persecutor who would "speak great words against the "Most High" God and wear out the saints and think to change times and laws (Daniel 7:25).

Scholars agree that the author of Daniel was alluding to the contemporary Hellenistic ruler of Palestine, Antiochus IV Epiphanes, who attempted to extirpate Judaism. But because Antiochus was not named, later readers could apply the prediction in Daniel to any persecutor. Early Christians applied it to the Roman emperors who persecuted the church, in particular Nero (reigned 54–68 CE).

Britannica Quiz, World Religions & Traditions

The four books of the New Testament that fueled the Christian belief in the Anti-Christ were the first two epistles of John, the Revelation to John, and the Second Letter of Paul to the Thessalonians. The first three of these were written near the end of the 1st century CE; the last was written either by St. Paul the Apostle shortly after 50 CE or by one of Paul's immediate disciples some 20 or 30 years later.

Neither 2nd Thessalonians nor Revelation uses the term Antichrist, but both works refer to a coming persecutor who is evidently the same person.

Differences between the Anti-Christ and an anti-Christs

The apostle John, among other writers in the New Testament, mentions certain characteristics of the anti-Christ. In the first place, there is the Anti-Christ with a capital "A." There were also many anti-Christ's in the world at the time of the New Testament church with a lower-case "a."

What is the difference between these two? Did the writers of the New Testament make a mistake in their choosing between a lower-case "a" and an upper-case "A?"

No, they were simply pointing out that anyone that opposes, for example, the divinity of Christ is an anti-Christ. There are many out there today who are anti-Christ's in that they deny the deity of Jesus Christ who is God (John 1).

Unbelievably, many who graduate from seminary deny that Jesus was fully God and fully man. These, by definition, are anti-Christ's. Atheists could be said to be anti-Christ because they do not believe in God and thus Jesus Christ as God and so they stand condemned (John 3:18).

The anti-Christ is not one person but a spirit of anti-Christ and so we know that there are many anti-Christ's but it is the spirit of anti-Christ that lives within humans and not a specific person (2 John 4:3).

In 1 John 2:18 John makes a distinction regarding the anti-Christ as he wrote, "Children, it is the last hour, and as you have heard that antichrist is coming, so now many antichrists have come. Therefore, we know that it is the last hour." Here John states that there are many anti-Christ's and that "you have heard that anti-Christ is coming."

John continues in verse 22, "Who is the liar? It is whoever denies that Jesus is the Christ. Such a person is the anti-Christ-denying the Father and the Son." Here again the identity of the lower-case anti-Christ is anyone who denies that Jesus is the Christ.

The Christ means the "***anointed One of God***." As John says, whoever denies Jesus as the Christ, or as the Messiah, denies the Father and the Son and this person and these people are the anti-Christ's." There are many anti-Christ's out there today just as there were in John's Day. But the anti-Christ is not the same as the Anti-Christ, upper-case "A." The world has no shortage of anti-Christs.

Their characteristics are that they also deny his virgin birth, his resurrection, his living a sinless life, and that he will return again to judge the world. For the believer, he will come as their King. For those who reject his gospel, he will come as their Judge (Rev 20). Either way, everyone will bow the knee and acknowledge Jesus Christ as Lord.as a condemned sinner or a resurrected and glorified saint (Rom 14:11, Phil 2:10).

The Number 666
(The Number of The Beast)

As anyone who is a new Bible student quickly learns, the meaning of **six hundred sixty-six** (666) is derived from the number and mark of the Beast Power discussed in the book of Revelation. The number 666 symbolizes the perfection of man's overall system that is separated from God and under the constant influence of Satan, the devil.

The number 666 is based on a Hebrew system of numerology called "Gematria" and refers to the sinfulness of man, as well as the rise of

the "Beast," or Satan, as Jesus Christ prepares to return to earth. It is mentioned in the last book of the New Testament, "Revelation."

Gematria is a system of numerology in which every letter of the Hebrew alphabet is assigned a numerical value and special meaning. For example, the number one refers to God who is complete in and of himself. Seven is the number of completion because the Bible states that God created the world in seven days. Six is one less than seven and is therefore incomplete. Human beings were also made on the sixth day of creation. Because Adam and Eve disobeyed God, choosing to sin by doing what God forbade them to do, the number six is also associated with sin, particularly the sinful nature of human beings.

It was Satan, or the devil (in the form of a snake), who enticed Eve into sinning and she enticed Adam, so sin has long been associated with Satan. The Book of Revelation describes the last gasps of Satan, who has, since the beginning of time, sought to take over the world. Revelation 13:18 states: "Here is wisdom. Let him that hath understanding count the number of the beast: for it is the number of a man; and his number is Six hundred threescore and six." This is the King James Version and "threescore" is an archaic English version of 60. So, 666 is the sign of the devil because the number six represents sin and man's incompleteness.

The Characteristics of the Anti-Christ

Paul spoke of one man as being the man of lawlessness (2 Thessalonians 2:3-4). Since we know the difference between the many anti-Christs and the Anti-Christ, let's look at Scripture to identify ten characteristics of the Anti-Christ.

Some theologians say that there are up to 37 characteristics of the Anti-Christ so we know that there are more than ten but we will only look at the most obvious of these ten, although you may think of different ones other than those mentioned here.

He Will Blaspheme God

Many of these same characteristics of the one Anti-Christ are also held by the many anti-Christ's. One of the greatest of these characteristics is that he will blaspheme the holy name of God. In Revelation 13:6 it says, "And he opened his mouth in blasphemies against God, to blaspheme his name and his tabernacle, that is, those who dwell in heaven."

Many who are unbelievers blaspheme God too when they use God's name as a swear word. This includes the vain use of Jesus' name as it is written in Exodus 20:7 (and several other places), "You shall not misuse the name of the LORD your God, for the LORD will not hold anyone guiltless who misuses his name." In fact, Jesus warned that every idle word that men and women speak they will have to give an account for in the Day of Judgment. Let that sink in, every idle word! That includes every word that is used with God's name in useless, vain or even casual speaking like "Oh my God!"

He will Claim to be God and is Worshiped

A strong characteristic is that the Anti-Christ will seek to be worshipped like God. Paul writes, "Let no man deceive you by any means: for that day shall not come, except there come a falling away first, and that man of sin be revealed, the son of perdition; Who opposes and exalts himself above all that is called God, or that is worshipped; so that he as God sits in the temple of God, shewing himself that he is God. "(2 Thessalonians 2:3-4).

This Anti-Christ is identified as the "man of lawlessness" and will not appear until the "rebellion" occurs (Rev 17). This man is supposed to come to power during the Tribulation and he will sit in the temple of God to proclaim himself as God.

He Will Display Miraculous Powers

Paul knew that this man of lawlessness would dazzle those who are deceived and that is why many will worship him. In 2 Thessalonians 2:9-12 Paul writes that "The coming of the lawless one will be in accordance with how Satan works. He will use all sorts of displays of power through signs and wonders that serve the lie, and all the ways that wickedness deceives those who are perishing.

They perish because they refused to love the truth. For this reason, God sends them a powerful delusion so that they will believe the lie and so that all will be condemned who have not believed the truth but have delighted in wickedness." The sad fact is that people will be so far removed from knowing Jesus Christ that they won't recognize the true God from the false one.

These powers are also mentioned in Revelation 13:13 as he "performed great signs, even causing fire to come down from heaven, to the earth in full view of the people." The difference is Jesus never performed miracles to draw attention to Himself but to glorify God. The Anti-Christ will try and draw glory to himself with miracles. (John 4:48)

The Anti-Christ Will Come Back to Life

Just like Jesus Christ died on the cross and was resurrected, the Anti-Christ will recover from what was considered a mortal wound. After this happened, he "ordered them to set up an image in honor of the beast who was wounded by the sword and yet lived" (Rev 13:14). What a feat that will cause many to be motivated by the sight of this "fatal wound", that had been healed; so much so that many will worship him (Rev 13:12).

This is imitating Jesus Christ again for even the disciple Thomas doubted that Jesus could recover from the death at his crucifixion but when he saw the resurrected Christ, he confirmed that Jesus was Lord and God (John 20:28).

The Anti-Christ Will Rule in Full Authority

The Anti-Christ, again mimicking Jesus' sovereignty, will rule for 42 months over the earth. For three and a half years he "was given authority to continue [literally "make war"] for forty-two months" (Rev 13:5). In fact the Anti-Christ "was given authority over every tribe, people, language and nation" (Rev 13:7). Christians know who actually reigns supreme for Jesus is Lord of all and has been given all authority in heaven and on earth. The Anti-Christ thinks he has power but he is given only as much power as God allows him to have. All this man's power is within the sovereign plan of God as God can even use evil for good.

The Anti-Christ Will Control the World's Economy

Whoever rules the world's goods rules the unsaved world. This man will have "forced all people, great and small, rich and poor, free and slave, to receive a mark on their right hands or on their foreheads, so that they could not buy or sell unless they had the mark, which is the name of the beast or the number of its name" (Rev 13:16-17).

When people start getting hungry, they will do almost anything to keep from starving. Even submit to an ungodly ruler. He causes everyone to receive a mark so that they can't even buy food or any goods at all unless they have his mark upon them. This is also mimicking the sovereign God who gives to all, great and small, the sustenance to survive. The Anti-Christ makes everyone receive his mark but this mark comes with a great price. Those who reject the mark are put to death.

The Anti-Christ Will Desecrate God's Temple

Daniel 11:31 mentions this abomination of desolation as his "armed forces will rise up to desecrate the temple fortress and will abolish the daily sacrifice. Then they will set up the abomination that causes desolation."

The "daily sacrifice is abolished" (Dan 12:11). He cannot be trusted because "He will invade the kingdom when its people feel secure and he will seize it through intrigue.

Then an overwhelming army will be swept away before him; both it and a prince of the covenant will be destroyed. After coming to an agreement with him, he will act deceitfully, and with only a few people he will rise to power. When the richest provinces feel secure, he will invade them and will achieve what neither his fathers nor his forefathers did. He will distribute plunder, loot and wealth among his followers. He will plot the overthrow of fortresses-but only for a time" (Dan 11:21-24). He is a liar and a thief of thieves. He makes an agreement and promises peace but then breaks his promise and deceives many.

Jesus spoke about this saying, "Therefore, when you see the abomination of desolation spoken of by Daniel the prophet, standing in the holy place' (whoever reads, let him understand), then let those who are in Judea flee to the mountains, Let him who is on the housetop not go down to take anything out of his house. And let him who is in the field not to back to get his clothes. "But woe to those who are pregnant and to those who are nursing babies in those days! And pray that your flight may not be in winter or on the Sabbath, For then there will be great tribulation, such as has not been since the beginning of the world until this time, no nor ever shall be" (Matt 24:15-21)

The Anti-Christ Will Attempt to Destroy Israel

Satan and all of those under his rule have always sought the destruction of the Jews. The end times see this brought to fruition. In Daniel 11:40-41 it says, "And at the time of the end shall the king of the south push at him: and the king of the north shall come against him like a whirlwind, with chariots, and with horsemen, and with many ships; and he shall enter into the countries, and shall overflow and pass over. He shall enter also into the glorious land [Jerusalem], and many [countries] shall be overthrown: but these shall escape out of his hand, [even] Edom, and Moab, and the chief of the children of Ammon."

This happens after another treaty is broken. At first, he promises to help be Jerusalem's savior but he, as always, is a liar and the truth is not in him (Dan 9:27). He breaks one treaty after another and makes one promise after another, breaking them all. It is obvious that his power comes from the father of lies, the Devil.

The Anti-Christ Will Cause Earth's Armies to Fight Against Christ

The Anti-Christ makes an unwise decision, showing that pride comes before the fall and what a great fall this is. John records that he "saw the beast and the kings of the earth and their armies gathered together to wage war against the rider on the horse and his army" (Rev 19:19). He is so deluded by power and by pride that he actually believes that he can even defeat Jesus Christ but he sorely miscalculates (Rev 19:20-21). Power not only corrupts but it also blinds a person to logic and common sense. What makes this man think that he can destroy God Almighty in the Person of Jesus Christ!?

That will be the last decision that Anti-Christ makes and it will be a fatal one for he is cast alive into the lake of fire where he can deceive the nations no more.

All Anti-Christ's Final Destiny

All of the little "a" anti-Christ's and the Anti-Christ are ultimately headed to one place; the lake of fire. If you are denying Jesus Christ is God and that he came in the flesh and lived a perfect, sinless life, that he died for sinners, and was raised again and today sits at the right hand of God, and that he is coming again to judge the world in righteousness, then you are also an anti-Christ (little "a"). There is nothing that is not forgivable except not believing in Jesus Christ as the Son of God (1 John 1:9). If you do not believe in

Jesus Christ then you are an anti-Christ and you stand condemned before God unless you repent (John 3:18).

There is still time to repent if you are reading this. If not, I hate to tell you the bad news of your and the Anti-Christ's final destination. It is found in Revelation 20:19-20, "And I saw the beast, the kings of the earth, and their armies, gathered together to make war against him who sat on the horse and against his army.

Then the beast (Anti-Christ) was captured, and with him the false prophet who worked signs in his presence, by which he deceived those who received the mark of the beast and those who worshiped his image. These two were cast alive into the lake of fire burning with brimstone."

Question? Who is the "False Prophet"? Gotquestions.com gives a detailed report that is really on the mark. Here's what they say:

The false prophet of the end times is described in Revelation 13:11-15. He is also referred to as the "second beast" (Revelation 13:11; 16:13, 19:20, 20:10). Together with the Antichrist and Satan, who empowers both of them, the false prophet is the third party in the unholy trinity.

The apostle John describes this person and gives us clues to identifying him when he shows up. *First*, he comes out of the earth. This could mean he comes up from the pit of hell with all the demonic powers of hell at his command. It could also mean he comes from lowly circumstances, secret and unknown until he bursts on the world stage at the right hand of the Anti-Christ.

He is depicted as having horns like a lamb, while speaking like a dragon. The horns on lambs are merely small bumps on their heads until the lamb grows into a ram. Rather than having the Anti-Christ's multiplicity of heads and horns, showing his power and might and fierceness, the false prophet comes like a lamb, winsomely, with persuasive words that elicit sympathy and good will from others.

He may be an extraordinary preacher or orator whose demonically empowered words will deceive the multitudes. But he speaks like a dragon, which means his message is the message of a dragon. Revelation 12:9 identifies the dragon as the devil and Satan.

Verse 12 gives us the false prophet's mission on earth, which is to force humanity to worship the Antichrist. He has all the authority of the Anti-Christ because, like him, the false prophet is empowered by Satan.

It is not clear whether people are forced to worship the Antichrist or whether they are so enamored of these powerful beings that they fall for the deception and worship him willingly. The fact that the second beast uses miraculous signs and wonders, including fire from heaven, to establish the credibility of both of them would seem to indicate that people will fall before them in adoration of their power and message. Verse 14 goes on to say the deception will be so great that the people will set up an idol to the Anti-Christ, "the image of the beast," and worship it.

This is reminiscent of the huge golden image of Nebuchadnezzar (Daniel 3) before which all were to bow down and pay homage. Revelation 14:9-11, however, describes the ghastly fate that awaits those who worship the image of the Anti-Christ.

Those who survive the terrors of the tribulation to this point will be faced with two hard choices. Those who refuse to worship the image of the beast will be subject to death (Revelation 13:15), but those who do worship him will incur the wrath of God.

The image will be extraordinary in that it will be able to "speak." Whatever the image is (a statue? a hologram? an android? a human-animal hybrid? a clone?), it will have some kind of ability to breathe forth the message of the Anti-Christ and the false prophet. Along with being the spokesman for them, the image will condemn to death those who refuse to worship the unholy pair. In our technological world, it is not hard to imagine such a scenario.

Whoever the false prophet turns out to be, the final world deception and the final apostasy will be great, and the whole world will be caught up in it. The deceivers and false teachers we see today are the forerunners of the Anti-Christ and the false prophet, and we must not be deceived by them.

These false teachers abound, and they are moving us toward a final satanic kingdom. We must faithfully proclaim the saving gospel of Jesus Christ and rescue the souls of men and women from the coming disaster.

Notice that they were cast into the lake of fire alive! Now, the good news means nothing unless we tell you the bad news first.

So now the good news (Rom 10:9-13). You don't have to go there (Acts 4:12). Since Christ has not yet returned, he is still waiting for some to repent. He is not willing that any perish apart from his saving grace (Acts 16:30-31).

I beg you to come to him and place your trust in the Savior, but if not, you will face him as Judge. My prayer is that you trust him today with your eternal destiny and place your faith in the only one who can save you. Jesus Christ who died for you.

Excerpts from Gotquestions.com.

(Read more: https://www.whatchristianswanttoknow.com/ten-characteristics-of-the-anti-christ-according-to-the-bible/#ixzz7sgYQqfpJ)

Author's Note: So, there will be a time in the near future that "The Anti-Christ" will appear and be seated as the God of Israel. He will be the full embodiment of Satan in human flesh, the incarnation of evil, if you will.

However, as we wait for the return of Jesus, we still have to deal with all those anti-Christ that do the bidding of the devil every day. These folks are immoral, self-centered, lustful and anti-God. They live for themselves and act as though they are their own god.

Hear what the Apostle John told the 1st century believers:

"Beloved, believe not every spirit, but try the spirits whether they are of God: because many false prophets are gone out into the world. Hereby know ye the Spirit of God: Every spirit that confesses that Jesus Christ is come in the flesh is of God:

And every spirit that confesses not that Jesus Christ is come in the flesh is not of God: and this is that spirit of anti-Christ, whereof ye have heard that it should come; and even now already is in the world.

Ye are of God, little children, and have overcome them: because greater is he that is in you, than he that is in the world. They are of the world: therefore, speak they of the world, and the world heareth them." I John 4:1-5

Did you get it? The Holy Spirit dwells in us because we are "Born Again" and he is greater than all the little anti-Christs that are running around this earth causing havoc.

These little anti-Christ reject Jesus as God in the flesh. They may see Jesus as a prophet or religious leader but for the most part they do not follow his teachings or hold fast to sound Biblical doctrine.

CHAPTER FOUR:
OUR WAITING POSTURE & PERSPECTIVES

As followers of Jesus, we have been given specific instructions while we wait for the return of our Lord. Let's look at some of them.

With regard to these little anti-Christs… "For we wrestle not against flesh and blood, but against principalities, against powers, against the rulers of the darkness of this world, against spiritual wickedness in high places." Ephesians 6:12

Our fight is not with people, even though they are anti-Christs. They are deceived and led by the devil or worse, their own sinful nature. Our fight is a fight of faith to believe the Word of God and use it against our adversary.

Peter said, "Be sober, be vigilant; because your adversary the devil, as a roaring lion, walketh about, seeking whom he may devour: whom resist steadfast in the faith, knowing that the same afflictions are accomplished in your brethren that are in the world." I Peter 5:8-9

With regard to ourselves…."And be not drunk with wine, wherein is excess; but be filled with the Spirit; Speaking to yourselves in psalms and hymns and spiritual songs, singing and making melody in your heart to the Lord; Giving thanks always for all things unto God and the Father in the name of our Lord Jesus Christ; Submitting yourselves one to another in the fear of God." Ephesians 5:18-21

Being filled with the Spirit is paramount because you cannot walk in or live in the Spirit if you are not filled with his presence. The ability to sing, give thanks and be happy is all predicated on a close relationship with the Lord.

The term, "Be Filled" is an action verb that says in effect, "Be Continually Filled" moment by moment…not just once in a lifetime.

"What? know ye not that your body is the temple of the Holy Ghost which is in you, which ye have of God, and ye are not your own? For ye are bought with a price: (The Blood of Jesus) therefore, glorify God in your body, and in your spirit, which are God's." I Corinthians 6:19-20

With regard to our Faith…(For we walk by faith, not by sight:) II Corinthians 5:7 Here are a few other scriptures that offer guidance and direction.

1. "But without faith it is impossible to please him: for he that cometh to God must believe that he is, and that he is a rewarder of them that diligently seek him." Hebrews 11:6
2. "So then faith cometh by hearing, and hearing by the word of God." Romans 10:17
3. "Now faith is the substance of things hoped for, the evidence of things not seen." Hebrews 11:1
4. "For therein is the righteousness of God revealed from faith to faith: as it is written, the just shall live by faith." Romans 1:17
5. "For by grace are ye saved through faith; and that not of yourselves: it is the gift of God: Not of works, lest any man should boast." Ephesians 2:8-9
6. "And Jesus said unto them, Because of your unbelief: for verily I say unto you, If ye have faith as a grain of mustard seed, ye shall say unto this mountain, Remove hence to yonder place; and it shall remove; and nothing shall be impossible unto you." Matthew 17:20
7. "I am crucified with Christ: nevertheless, I live; yet not I, but Christ lives in me: and the life which I now live in the flesh I live by the faith of the Son of God, who loved me, and gave himself for me." Galatians 2:20
8. "For whatsoever is born of God overcomes the world: and this is the victory that overcomes the world, even our faith." I John 5:4

9. "Not for that we have dominion over your faith, but are helpers of your joy: for by faith ye stand." II Corinthians 1:24
10. "Looking unto Jesus the author and finisher of our faith; who for the joy that was set before him endured the cross, despising the shame, and is set down at the right hand of the throne of God." Hebrews 12:2

There are over 90 scriptures that mention or imply faith. The above scriptures are certainly enough to support my premise that while we are waiting, we need to be busy about our Father's work.

With regard to being ready…"Watch therefore: for ye know not what hour your Lord doth come." Matthew 24:42

Being ready is very important. I remember when I was a young Christian, I still smoked and when we discussed Jesus coming back, I thought about grabbing an extra pack of cigarettes, just to be sure. 60-years later, I know that was foolish thinking. However, what can we do to be ready? We must watch and pray always to be sure we are prepared to meet our Lord.

With regard to daily living…"Let not your heart be troubled: ye believe in God, believe also in me. In my Father's house are many mansions: if it were not so, I would have told you. I go to prepare a place for you. And if I go and prepare a place for you, I will come again, and receive you unto myself; that where I am, there ye may be also." John 14:1-3

As we go through our daily routine waiting for Jesus to return, we may very well pass through the valley of shadows, even the valley of death. But the good news is, the Lord is always with us. In fact, he even prepares a feast for us in the presence of our enemies (the little anti-Christs). He even anoints our heads with oil. There is no reason to fear. See why in the 23rd Psalm.

"The LORD is my shepherd; I shall not want. He makes me to lie down in green pastures: he leadeth me beside the still waters. He restoreth my soul: he leadeth me in the paths of righteousness for his name's sake.

Yea, though I walk through the valley of the shadow of death, I will fear no evil: for thou art with me; thy rod and thy staff they comfort me. Thou preparest a table before me in the presence of my enemies: thou anoint my head with oil; my cup runs over. Surely goodness and mercy shall follow me all the days of my life: and I will dwell in the house of the LORD forever."

Paul told the church at Rome, "**If God** be for **us, who can be against us**? He that spared not his own Son, but delivered him up for **us** all, how shall he not with him also freely give **us** all things? Who shall lay anything to the charge of **God**'s elect? It is **God** that justifies" Romans 8:31-33

"Nay, in all these things we are more than conquerors through him that loved us. For I am persuaded, that neither death, nor life, nor angels, nor principalities, nor powers, nor things present, nor things to come, nor height, nor depth, nor any other creature, shall be able to separate us from the love of God, which is in Christ Jesus our Lord." Romans 8:37-39

"**I am crucified with Christ:** nevertheless, I live; yet not I, but Christ lives in me: and the life which I now live in the flesh, I live by the faith of the Son of God, who loved me, and gave himself for me." Galatians 2:20-21

"Let your light so shine before men, that they may see your good works and glorify your Father in heaven." Matthew 5:16

Our waiting posture should be one of a shining light. But not of our self-willed energy. Instead, the fruit of the Spirit (Galatians 5:22) is the source of our light.

With **regard to having peace…** He is in control. The battle is really his. I dedicated chapter seven to resting in the Lord. I think it will be most helpful as we wait for Jesus to return.

CHAPTER FIVE:

FALSE CHRISTIANS & RELIGIONS

We discovered in chapter four that this world is full of little anti-Christs. Many of them are running our government, teaching our kids in schools, are movie stars, doctors, lawyers and lots of other occupations.

It's easy to recognize those that are followers of a false religion. They openly teach against Jesus and lead many astray with their humanistic or social gospel. Check out my book, "How To Recognize False Religions, Doctrines and Teachings" for a more complete overview.

False Christians are another matter. They are not so easy to spot. They can talk the talk and walk the walk but are not really, "Born Again" as Jesus said. They get into our churches and slowly manipulate until a doctrine is changed or and Christian principle is compromised.

Did you know that many Christian churches now accept homosexuals? Their open and aggressive stand against the Biblical teachings on marriage are flaunted in the face of weak believers. The church overlooks the scriptures that condemn such a practice. Read it for yourself:

"For the wrath of God is revealed from heaven against all ungodliness and unrighteousness of men, who hold the truth in unrighteousness; Because that which may be known of God is manifest in them; for God hath shewed it unto them.

For the invisible things of him from the creation of the world are clearly seen, being understood by the things that are made, even his eternal power and Godhead; so that they are without excuse: Because that, when they knew God, they glorified him not as God, neither were thankful; but became vain in their imaginations, and their foolish heart was darkened.

Professing themselves to be wise, they became fools, and changed the glory of the uncorruptible God into an image made like to corruptible man, and to birds, and four-footed beasts, and creeping things.

Wherefore God also gave them up to uncleanness through the lusts of their own hearts, to dishonor their own bodies between themselves: Who changed the truth of God into a lie, and worshipped and served the creature more than the Creator, who is blessed forever. Amen.

For this cause God gave them up unto vile affections: for even their women did change the natural use into that which is against nature: And likewise, also the men, leaving the natural use of the woman, burned in their lust one toward another; men with men working that which is unseemly, and receiving in themselves that recompense of their error.

And even as they did not like to retain God in their knowledge, God gave them over to a reprobate mind, to do those things which are not convenient; Being filled with all unrighteousness, fornication, wickedness, covetousness, maliciousness; full of envy, murder, debate, deceit, malignity; whisperers, backbiters, haters of God, despiteful, proud, boasters, inventors of evil things, disobedient to parents, without understanding, covenant breakers, without natural affection, implacable, unmerciful: Who knowing the judgment of God, that they which commit such things are worthy of death, not only do the same, but have pleasure in them that do them." Romans 1:18-32

It is obvious, from the above scriptures, that Gays, Lesbians, By-Sexual and Transvestites (LGBT) are not just an alternate lifestyle but rather a direct rejection of the true and living God and a manifestation of SIN.

This is not my personal opinion. It is what the Bible says about the matter. This is what we, as Christians, must turn away from and above all never allow in our membership without repentance and careful review to be sure demonic influences are no longer present.

A false Christian is one that does not adhere to the doctrines of the Bible that delineate Christianity. Here's a good example:

"O foolish Galatians, who hath bewitched you, that ye should not obey the truth, before whose eyes Jesus Christ hath been evidently set forth, crucified among you?

This only would I learn of you, received ye the Spirit by the works of the law, or by the hearing of faith? Are ye so foolish? having begun in the Spirit, are ye now made perfect by the flesh? Have ye suffered so many things in vain? if it be yet in vain.

He therefore that ministers to you the Spirit, and worketh miracles among you, doeth he it by the works of the law, or by the hearing of faith? Even as Abraham believed God, and it was accounted to him for righteousness. Know ye therefore that they which are of faith, the same are the children of Abraham. And the scripture, foreseeing that God would justify the heathen through faith, preached before the gospel unto Abraham, saying, in thee shall all nations be blessed.

So then, they which be of faith are blessed with faithful Abraham. For as many as are of the works of the law are under the curse: for it is written, cursed is every one that continues not in all things which are written in the book of the law to do them.

But that no man is justified by the law in the sight of God, it is evident: for, the just shall live by faith. And the law is not of faith: but, the man that doeth them shall live in them. Christ hath redeemed us from the curse of the law, being made a curse for us: for it is written, cursed is every one that hangs on a tree: That the blessing of Abraham might come on the Gentiles through Jesus Christ; that we might receive the promise of the Spirit through faith." Galatians 3:3-14

This group of 1st century believers started out in the Spirit but ended up in the flesh. They reverted back to the laws of Moses as a foundation for their salvation. Instead of walking by faith, they embraced the rules and regulations of the Jewish religion.

Paul tells the church in another letter that, "For by grace are ye saved through faith; and that not of yourselves: it is the gift of God: Not of works, lest any man should boast. For we are his workmanship, created in Christ Jesus unto good works, which God hath before ordained that we should walk in them." Ephesians 2:8-10

Our salvation has always been by Grace through faith, not works. "Jesus answered and said unto them, this is the work of God, that ye believe on him whom he hath sent." John 6:29

Many Christian churches have strayed from the truth of the Gospel. Look at the PEW report of Religious Beliefs in the US.

Over the last few decades, the proportion of the U.S. population that is white Christian has declined by nearly one-third. As recently as 1996, almost two-thirds of Americans (65%) identified as white and Christian. By 2006, that had declined to 54%, and by 2017 it was down to 43%. The proportion of white Christians hit a low point in 2018, at 42%, and rebounded slightly in 2019 and 2020, to 44%. That tick upward indicates the decline is slowing from its pace of losing roughly 11% per decade.

Non-practicing Christians have grown from 35% to 43% from 2000 to 2020. During the same time, practicing Christians declined from 45% to 25%. Non-Christians or agnostic rose from 20% to 32%.

People are much less confident in the divinity of Jesus. Most adults—not quite six in 10—believe Jesus was God **(56%),** while about one-quarter say he was only a religious or spiritual leader like Mohammed or the Buddha (26%).

The Vast Majority of Americans Believe Jesus Was a Real Person

Jesus Christ has made a cameo in hundreds of pop culture places, from The *Da Vinci Code* to *South Park*. But, although the character of Jesus has certainly been fictionalized, satirized and mythologized over the centuries, the vast majority of Americans still maintain that he was a historical figure.

More than nine out of 10 adults say Jesus Christ was a real person who actually lived (92%). While the percentages dip slightly among younger generations—only 87 percent of Millennials agree Jesus actually lived—

Americans are still very likely to believe the man, Jesus Christ, once walked the earth.

Millennials are the only generation among whom fewer than half believe Jesus was God (48%). About one-third of young adults (35%) say instead that Jesus was merely a religious or spiritual leader, while 17 percent aren't sure what he was.

In each older generation, the belief in Jesus as divine is more common—55 percent of Gen-Xers, 58 percent of Boomers and nearly two-thirds of Elders (62%) believe Jesus was God. That's still a lot that do not believe at all.

Americans Are Divided on Whether Jesus Was Sinless. Perhaps reflective of their questions about Jesus' divinity, Americans are conflicted on whether Jesus committed sins during his earthly life. About half of Americans agree, either strongly or somewhat, that while he lived on earth, Jesus Christ was human and committed sins like other people (52%). Just less than half disagree, either strongly or somewhat, that Jesus committed sins while on earth (46%), and 2 percent aren't sure.

Similar to other trends in perceptions of Jesus, Millennials are more likely to believe Jesus committed sins while he was on earth—56% of Millennials believe so. Gen-Xers, Boomers and Elders are all similar to the national average when it comes to beliefs about Jesus' fallibility—they are almost evenly split on whether Jesus sinned while he lived on earth.

Most Americans Say They Have Made a Commitment to Jesus Christ.

On the whole, America is still committed to Jesus. The act of making a personal commitment to Jesus—often seen as the "first step" in becoming a Christian—is a step that more than six in 10 Americans say they have taken and, moreover, that commitment is still important in their life today.

While the majority of Americans report such a commitment, some groups are significantly more likely to have done so than others. Women, for example, are more likely than men to have made a personal commitment to Jesus (68% compared to 56%, respectively).

Millennials are much less likely than any other group to have made a personal commitment to Jesus that is still important in their life today. Fewer than half of Millennials say they have made such a commitment (46%), compared to six in 10 Gen-Xers (59%), two-thirds of Boomers (65%) and seven in 10 Elders (71%).

People Are Conflicted between "Jesus" and "Good Deeds" as the Way to Heaven. Among adults who have made a personal commitment to Jesus, most also believe that Jesus is the way to heaven. When given several beliefs about the afterlife to choose from, nearly two-thirds of those who have made a personal commitment to Jesus say they believe that after they die, they will go to heaven because they have confessed their sins and accepted Jesus Christ as their savior (63%). Only 2 percent of adults who report a personal commitment to Jesus say they will not go to heaven. About one in seven admit they don't know what will happen after they die (15%).

Overall, roughly two out of five Americans have confessed their sinfulness and professed faith in Christ (a group Barna classifies as "born again Christians").

Many adults believe, however, that they will go to heaven as a result of their good works. Broadly speaking, this is the most common perception among Americans who have never made a commitment to Jesus—and it is also quite common among self-identified Christians. In this category, people believe they will go to heaven because they have tried to obey the Ten Commandments (5%), as a result of being basically a good person (8%), or on the grounds that God loves all people and will not let them perish (7%).

Why all the statistics? Simple, so you can see the condition of the church. Their beliefs are all over the place. 44% do not believe Jesus was God in the flesh. If this is not a falling away, I don't now what is.

A false Christian is one who says he or she is a Christian but was never, "Born Again." The Church is slowly trending toward a unity that excludes personal faith and fundamental doctrines. Instead, they follow salvation by works, acceptance of immoral open sin among members and a general lack of Godliness.

Jesus said that there would be a falling away from faith before he returns.

It's happening now in our lifetime. The Bible says it will keep declining. We must hold fast to our faith and walk with Jesus every day.

CHAPTER SIX:
WHAT SOME FOLKS THINK ABOUT GOD

The Atheist, of course, believes that there is no God. They follow an evolutionary path that leads into the grave with no afterlife. Their purpose for living is not defined and the meaning of life is unsure. They live for today and usually for themselves.

The Jehovah's Witness, believe that Jesus was really Michael, the archangel, that there is no Trinity, that salvation is obtained by a combination of faith, good works, and obedience, not grace as the Bible says and God is not personal in any way.

The Mormons, Latter Day Saints, believe that Jesus was really Adam, that there is no one eternal God, that men, not women, can attain a god status and dwell in the heavens with other exalted men in a counsel of gods… That these exalted men-gods become the god of their own world.

The New Age Movement, for the most part believes in a Pantheistic view of god. This is to say that God is everything and everything is God. There are no personal relationship possibilities, only the belief that the individual is God because God is everything including all human beings.

The Muslims believe that Allah is god but Allah is the name of the Moon-god that Mohamed chose from many other gods in his day to lead his followers into a belief of only one God. Allah is not Jehovah, the God of the Bible. In-fact, Allah can be traced back to the days of King David and the philistines and their false god, Baal.

WICCA, An Association of Occultic Groups, believes that god is "the mother goddess" and her companion "the horned god," who manifest themselves in Nature. This loosely knit association includes such groups as Neo-Pagans, Witches, Mediums, Sorcery, Satanism and more.

Universalism believes in any concept of God you feel is right, not what the Bible teaches. They are also an association of sorts including Buddhist, Hindu, Humanist, Jewish, Muslim, Pagan, atheist and agnostic. They do not believe in the Trinity or the Incarnation of Christ.

We, as Christians, believe In Jehovah, the one and only true and living God. All other beliefs related to gods are false. We also believe in the Incarnation of Christ, the atonement, Salvation by grace, the 2nd coming of Christ and the resurrection of Jesus from the dead.

Folks believe some strange stuff. When you say, do you believe in God? You will get a lot of, "Yeses" but odds are there will be a radical re-definition of God to suite their belief system.

Will The Real God Please Stand Up?

How is it that there are so many different concepts of God? I would say it is because most of us create our own god to suite our specific needs.

We are in a world of "designer gods" fashioned for each occasion. It appears to me that all but one is an example of man reaching upward to an unknown entity. Because they do not know the God of the Bible. They make him up out of their imaginations or fears.

The only God that reaches down to us is the God of the Bible. He has revealed himself to man so we could know him; to redeem us from our own sin; to invite us to share in his kingdom; to love us as his own children.

Why does man reject so great a salvation? I guess it's like what the Bible says,

"And this is the condemnation, that light is come into the world, and men loved darkness rather than light, because their deeds were evil." John 3:19

What Do Folks Believe About Jesus?

The Jehovah's Witnesses believe that Jesus is Michael, the archangel and that the Mormons believe that Jesus is Adam.

We already know that Atheists do not believe in God so Jesus would be out of their belief system too.

We know that all the "isms" follow a pantheistic view of God or like some Eastern Religions, a polytheistic belief in many gods. In all of these there is no room for Jesus.

Only Christianity believes that Jesus is the only begotten Son of God. (John 3:16)

Only Christianity believes that Jesus was and still is the 2nd person of a triune God that was with God from the beginning and in due time came to dwell in human flesh…thus the Incarnation. (John 1:1-16)

Only Christianity believes that Jesus is the only way to God the Father; that there are not many roads that lead to eternal life but only one, through Jesus, the Christ, who was crucified on a Roman cross at Mt. Calvary. (John 14:6)

Remember what Jesus said, "Verily I say unto you, except ye be converted, and become as little children, ye shall not enter into the kingdom of heaven." Matthew 18:3

"Jesus answered and said unto him, Verily, verily, I say unto thee, except a man be born again, he cannot see the kingdom of God." John 3:3

All these folks will not be caught up into the air to meet Jesus at the rapture because they reject God's plan of salvation and distort the very image of God. Jesus is coming for his church, not false religious folks or fake Christians.

However, Jesus promised that he is coming back, and we are to comfort one another with these words. We are not to wait in terror, because, as believers, we have the hope of the coming again of Christ.

CHAPTER SEVEN:
RESTING IN THE LORD

This world is full of confusion, fear, restlessness, hate, worry and a lot of immorality. Living a happy Christian life can be very difficult. However, it can be done. It is all about resting in the Lord. While we wait for our Lord to return, we need to rest.

There is a rest that God has provided for his children. However, this rest is only for those who walk with the Lord by faith. If you are a sometimes Christian with very little Biblical knowledge, you will most likely miss out on God's rest.

What are we resting from? We are stopping the practice of unbelief. No longer are we to doubt God and his Lordship over our lives. That means no worry, no anxiety, no fear of the future, no concern about what tomorrow will bring. All of that stuff is now under God's control.

You cannot stumble into the rest of God. The Lord has to lead you there. That means you have to be tuned into hearing his voice and willing to obey his commands. Otherwise, you will stray off in another direction by yourself. God must, above all else, lead you. Now let's look at the scriptural support for such a notion.

Psalm 23 is probably the most well-known text in the Holy Scriptures. We have already talked about it but I mention it again to call it back to your attention so you again see the proper posture and the right perspective.

There was a time when every school child would learn it and say it as a daily routine. Sadly, those days are mostly gone because of our government's hatred of all things Godly. However, disdain for the Bible does not diminish the spiritual impact made by its words.

Some folks fear turning their lives over to God because he might lead them somewhere they do not want to go. The 23rd psalm tells us that being led by God is a rewarding experience. We end up in green pastures (Prosperity) and lie down by still waters (Peace-no confusion); Our souls (Mind, Will & Emotions) are restored; The fear of evil fades away; Goodness and mercy follow us through life; We even have a feast while our enemies look on and finally, we dwell with the Lord forever. That's a pretty good deal, don't you think? However:

God's Rest Is Not For Everyone

God does not lead the masses into his rest. He leads his children. He must be your shepherd. That makes you, his sheep. Being a sheep has certain indicators that prove you are really a sheep and not a wolf:

1. Sheep hear their Shepherd's voice.
2. Sheep come to their Shepherd's call.
3. Sheep do not question their Shepherd's commands.
4. Sheep know when the wolf is near and cries for the Shepherd.

The atheist, agnostic, pantheist all others that reject Jesus Christ, as well as disobedient Christians, do not and will not follow his lead. Thus, they miss out on God's rest.

The rest of God spoken of in scriptures is a blessing of fellowship and a benefit to only those that are fully persuaded that he (God) is able and willing to protect and guide them through life.

God's Promise of Rest Hebrews 4:1-11

"Therefore, since a promise remains of entering his rest, let us fear lest any of you seem to have come short of it. For indeed the gospel was preached to us as well as to them; but the word, which they heard did not profit them, not being mixed with faith in those who heard it. For we who have believed do enter that rest, as he has said: although the works were finished from the foundation of the world. So, I swore in my wrath, they shall not enter my rest, For he has spoken in a certain place of the seventh day in this way: "And God rested on the seventh day from all His works"; and again in this place: "They shall not enter my rest.

Since therefore it remains that some must enter it, and those to whom it was first preached did not enter because of disobedience, again he designates a certain day, saying in David, "Today," after such a long time, as it has been said: Today, if you will hear his voice, do not harden your hearts.

For if Joshua had given them rest, then he would not afterward have spoken of another day. There remains therefore a rest for the people of God. For he who has entered his rest has himself also ceased from his works as God did from his.

Let us therefore be diligent to enter that rest, lest anyone fall according to the same example of disobedience."

We are encouraged to rest from all our works because God rested from all his works. The promise from God is that we can really enter into his rest and because he did, we can too.

However, sometimes we have to labor to enter in. Why? Because we get so caught up in what we are doing that it becomes really hard to just sit back and leave it up to God.

Someone may be wondering what, "all our works" is. It is not getting up and going to work every day or being a reliable husband or wife.

The rest is from trying to attain salvation by our own efforts. God took care of that in his master plan before the foundation of the world. His redemptive plan for man was to sacrifice his only Son as a penalty for sin and offer his salvation to all who would believe. (John 3:16)

To rest then is to believe that Jesus was sacrificed for our sin and accept him as our savior. We are to put our trust in him and stop trying to buy God's favor with good works. (Ephesians 2:8-9)

That which we are to let go of is the anxiety, fear, confusion, worry and control over our own lives. We are to step off the throne of our life. That seat is now reserved for Jesus. We can trust him because he said from the cross; "It Is Finished" which fulfilled God's rest from all his works on the 7th day of creation. He already made plans for us to rest in him.

"God made him who had no sin to be sin for us, so that in him we might become the righteousness of God" (2 Corinthians 5:21). We can now cease from our spiritual labors and rest in him, not just one day a week, but every day.

Spiritually Speaking

Let's look at the spiritual applications of resting in the Lord. As Christians, we have made Jesus Lord and seek to walk with him through this life. However, evil is on every side and it is hard to live out our faith in Christ.

We strive to make ends meet. We worry over our children and their future. We hope that sickness or sorrow will not knock on our door. We are anxious, fearful, and when someone says to us, "How are you doing today", we reply with, "I am just hanging in there."

This is a word picture of a Christian without faith. They are doing just what the Old Testament saints did, not believing. Their unbelief kept them from entering into God's rest. We can fall into the same scenario and miss out on the promise.

How Do We Enter In?

Our labor to enter in is believing. What do we believe? We believe that God rested on the 7th day from all his work. That means his master plan was complete. It means that God saw every need, every situation and every prayer in his foreknowledge and scheduled them for action in his master plan.

The Law was seen long before it appeared. In the fullness of time, it came to expose sin and bring death to all that sin. (Lev.18:20) Accordingly, in the fullness of time, Christ came with a new law…the law of the Spirit of Life that brought us liberty and salvation. (Romans 8:2) This new law set us free from the old one. However, both were in God's master plan waiting to be released.

We are in God's master plan and he works everything together for our good and his glory. (Romans 8:28) All we have to do is trust in Jesus; believe that he is in control; and wait for the manifestation of our deliverance/supply.

We enter in by faith and we remain at rest by faith knowing that the battle is the Lords and he is our shield.

Jesus is our shield against evil and lack in this life. He will provide. He will lead us to green pastures and still waters. He will restore our souls.

Unbelieving Christians

The Bible tells us that some of the Old Testament saints did not believe and they perished in the wilderness. They never entered the rest of God that was promised to them. They never entered the "Promised Land." However, the amazing thing was that God still took care of them in the wilderness. Their shoes did not wear out. nor did their clothing. They ate manna from heaven. Not one was feeble in mind or spirit. They still died in the wilderness. Here's what this says to me:

Life can be good but you can still die in the wilderness

1. It is better to fear (reverence) God than to fear giants and men of power and authority that dwell in your future.

2. God's blessings are always connected with faith. No faith, no promise, no divine destiny.
3. Fear will hinder faith. They are both sides of the same coin. But faith crushes fear and brings victory.
4. One's destiny lies in his or her own hands. We choose the path to walk in life and what lies at the end of the road. Life or death is in the power of our own choices.
5. God is looking for partners to rule the earth and has chosen us, his children…those who are willing to stand with him.

Benefits of Entering Into God's Rest

1. We have continual access into God's rest where we find peace.
2. We gain a new perspective on life and eternity.
3. We do not beat ourselves up when we fall short.
4. We start being who we are in Christ and not what others think we are.
5. We have true fellowship with God and we rest in his grace.
6. We see God at work fighting our battles for us. The battle is the Lords.

As we rest in God, we grow in grace. We see his hand in our life and hear his voice. All of this makes us more thankful than ever before.

Our praise and adoration for God is because we know that "If it had not been the Lord", we would not have been able to stand.

I am sure you can find more benefits. Mine are just some that I know to be true.

It was Jesus that completed the Law and opened up the door of grace for those who believed in him. He was the one that lived the life that God expected us to live, a righteous life.

He was the only one that could die for the sins of mankind, because he was, as it were, the spotless Lamb of God, that was foreshadowed in the Hebrew sacrifices of the Old Testament. It was he that became the Captain of our Salvation and Lord of Heaven and Earth.

The only thing we are instructed to fear is unbelief. We always want to believe regardless of what we see or feel. God is always with us and he alone is in control. This is the perspective that should rule our lives and shape our actions. Unbelief has no place in our spiritual walk with Jesus. ***We walk by faith and not by sight.*** II Corinthians 5:7

There is one sure way to rest in the Lord while you are waiting for Jesus to return. It has to do with the daily practice of allowing the "Peace of God" to rule over everything that you do. Here's the text:

"Be careful (Anxious) for nothing; but in everything by prayer and supplication with thanksgiving **let** your requests be made known unto **God.** And the "P**eace of God**", which passes all understanding, shall keep your hearts and minds through Christ Jesus: Philippians 4:6-7

Peace is one of the attributes of God. It is listed in the list of the different fruits as described in Galatians 5:22. We can actually apply this scripture to our everyday lives by letting it rule over us.

If you do not have peace about going somewhere or doing something, drop it like a hot potato. If you are in the midst of a thing that is bringing you anxiety or fear, drop it and go back to God for clarity.

This simple practice can keep you in a posture of rest and help you overcome evil suggestions and temptations.

CHAPTER EIGHT:
WHAT YOU SHOULD KNOW

I want to focus now on specific foundational principles that will set you free if you are in any type of bondage, being physical, emotional or spiritual. These truths will keep you until Jesus comes again.

Christianity is not a religion. It is a *Walk With God*. It does not boil down to a set of rules and regulations that if broken cause punishment. It is a relationship between you and God.

Jesus said, "My sheep hear my voice, and I know them, and they follow me: And I give unto them eternal life; and they shall never perish, neither shall any man pluck them out of my hand." John 10:27-28

You are Loved And Accepted By God

Many churchgoers do not know in whom they have believed. Some even think that God is a mean old man, ready to strike out at any infraction, even if it is a small one. However, the Bible says that God is Love and Love is even listed as one of the fruits of His Spirit.

Set your mind to know that God is not mad at you. Tell yourself that he loves you and has your best interest at heart. This is a foundational principle that will bring you much joy and peace, knowing you are loved and accepted by your creator. See John 3:16 It doesn't matter what others think about you. All that matters is what God thinks about you…and he loves you.

The Devil Is An Evil Lying Spirit

Jesus said that He came to earth so we might have life and that life would be abundant. However, he also contrasts his mission with that of the thief/devil. He says, "The thief comes but to steal, kill and destroy". John 10:10. So we know that we are marked by the devil for burglary, death and destruction. Ignoring this is not smart. We need to know the tricks of our enemy and how to defeat him. Consider reading my other Book, "The Authority of The Believer." It is on my website, www.MarinelliChristianBooks.com

You Have Authority Over Evil Spirits

Peter tells us in I Peter 5:8-9 "Be sober, be vigilant; because your adversary the devil, as a roaring lion, walks about, seeking whom he may devour: Whom resist steadfast in the faith, knowing that the same afflictions are accomplished in your brethren that are in the world.

This tells me that the devil is defeated. He may roar like a lion and scare me at times but all I have to do is resist him in the faith and he will run away with his tail between his legs. If I understand this, I will have a mindset that grounds me in times of trouble. I can resist by quoting scriptures like Jesus did when he was tempted in the wilderness. I can stand on the known promises of God found in the Bible. Do this and you will have victory.

You Can Let The Peace of God Be The Referee

There are many situations in life that require our attention and decisions. We are always making choices. Do I do this or that? Which is right? Should I take this job or that one? Life's decisions go on and on. However, now we can find God's will in the matters at hand by applying one simple truth. Here's what the scripture says…

"And let the peace of God rule in your hearts, to the which also ye are called in one body; and be ye thankful." Colossians 3:15 One version actually says umpire or referee.

If the peace of God is allowed to referee, it will blow its whistle when you are off sides and call you back. You will know that you are making the wrong decision because you just do not have peace about it.

This mindset is a great weapon against temptation and intimidation from others. If you cannot find peace, drop it, no matter how important it seems at the time. It is not of God and he is telling you to stay away from it.

Confusion Is Not of God

"For God is not the author of confusion, but of peace, as in all churches of the saints." I Corinthians 14:33

Knowing this truth is essential to finding God's will and making good decisions. If you are confused, it is not of God. He does not author or cause confusion. He does author peace and seeks to help you to walk in it at all times. If you suffer under confusion, toss whatever you are confused about out and seek the Lord for his peace.

Fear Is Not from Your Heavenly Father.

"For *God* hath *not* given us the spirit of *fear*; but of power, and of love, and of a sound mind." II Timothy 1:7 Ask yourself this question…"If fear is not from God, who does it belong to?" Fear brings torment and the only spirit that uses it is evil. Thus, it should be crushed before it takes hold. You can do that by seeking the Lord for a sound mind.

All Things Will Work Together For Your Good.

"And we know that in all things God works for the good of those who love him, who have been called according to his purpose" Romans 8:28

God does not cause bad things to happen to us but he will cause them to work together for our benefit. If we have this mindset, we can go on, even in the midst of trouble, knowing that God is with us and is actively working behind it all so we are ultimately blessed.

I remember a man that was devastated because his marriage ended after many years. He was bitter and blamed God. Many years later, I ran into him and his new wife. He was so happy and said to me, "I couldn't see any good coming from my divorce back then when it happened but now, I can see how he worked it all out for my benefit."

There Must Be A Reason For That.

Have you ever wondered why things happen? Things like someone pulling out onto the highway right in front of you and then slowing down…or like you can't get your car started and are late for work…or having a meeting downtown and it is suddenly cancelled. Do things happen for a reason or are they just happenstance? Here's a real live example from the Bible. It's found in John 9:1-23

"Now as *Jesus* passed by, He saw a man who was blind from birth. And his disciples asked him, saying, "Rabbi, who sinned, this man or his parents, that he was born blind?"

Jesus answered, "Neither this man nor his parents sinned, but that the works of God should be revealed in him. I must work the works of him who sent me while it is day; *the* night is coming when no one can work. As long as I am in the world, I am the light of the world."

Did you get the picture? Jesus was walking by with his disciples and saw a blind man. His disciples wanted to know why this guy was blind from his birth. Jesus said it was because the works of God should be revealed in him. He was also careful to explain that it was not the guys' fault or his parents.

There is always a reason for what happens to us. The sovereignty of God was at play as God intervened in the blind man's life. You can bet your bottom dollar that when God steps in, he has a good reason for doing so.

Having this mindset keep you at peace because when frustration enters our day and we get irritated, we can return to our rest knowing that "There Must Be A Reason For That." It calls us to a posture of submission and invokes an attitude of patience as we wait upon the Lord.

Jesus Is Really Coming Soon

Jesus told his disciples that he would be crucified, buried and would rise from the dead. He also said that he would go to the Father and prepare a place for us. Finally, he told us that he would return to gather his followers unto himself.

Christians have been waiting ever since for his return. When that time comes, according to his own testimony, he will separate the sheep from the goats. Then he will invite his sheep to enter into his kingdom that was prepared for them before the foundation of the world. The goats, on the other hand, are to be banished from his sight into an everlasting hell fire.

The reason I added this to my list of foundational principles is because it could be in our lifetime. All the signs point to the fact that he is coming soon.

That one thought can be the inspiration to live a righteous life, in submission to his will, and to comfort ourselves, knowing that he will make all things right. That is to say, those that have hurt us will be punished. We will see their destruction. Good will always win, even if it is at the end of all things.

God's Angels Watch Over Us

Do you believe in angels? I know some folks that say they believe in angels but do not believe in God. Go figure! If angels exist, there has to be a God and if there is a God, there has to be a heaven where he dwells and life eternal because angels are eternal beings.

There is no convincing evidence in Scripture that every person has their own specific guardian angel. There are angels who protect, guard and minister to God's people (Ps. 91:11-12), but the wicked have no angels of God to protect and guide them. They have only demonic spirits that seek to torment them, kill their dreams, steel their peace and destroy their destiny.

Psalm 34:7 tells us that, "The angel of the LORD encamps round about them that fear him, and delivers them." The word, "fear" is also translated, "Reverence". If we reverence or worship God, he will send his own angel to set up a fully operational camp of warring angels. Their sole mission is to protect and deliver you.

Having this mindset is to rest in an upside-down world of hate, evil and other ungodly activities. We can thus relax, even in the midst of turmoil.

These "Fundamental Principles" make up one powerful mindset. They are the foundation upon which you build your faith and walk with God.

If you apply them, they will keep you in his will. They will keep you out of the snares of the devil, and they will help you to experience the joy of the Lord as never before.

If you ignore these "Foundational Principles", you will continue to stumble through life and be tossed to and frow by the turbulence of an ever-raging emotional sea that is full of confusion, fear, and a lot more.

God loves us and wants us to walk with him but he does not take prisoners. We must come to him freely and completely. Are you ready?

CHAPTER NINE:

BEING, "BORN AGAIN" IS ESSENTIAL

There is a great falling away from the faith in America. Many denominations do not even agree on Jesus being the only way to God. The gospel has been diluted into a "Social Gospel" that promotes the notion that every person is a child of God no matter what religion or denomination.

You Must Be "Born Again"

"Jesus answered and said unto him,
Verily, verily, I say unto thee, except
a man be born again, he cannot see
the kingdom of God". John 3:3

This false doctrine that everyone is a child of God drives our political, racial, and economic worlds so as to destroy the very fabric of true faith and Biblical truth. Instead of God being supreme, man has opted to become his own god.

This theological premise is not limited to the non-Christian world. It has also invaded the church. If you are surprised to learn these facts, let me share a few statistics from the PEW report, a well-known organization that tracts trends and movement in religion.

The PEW Research Report

This report says that 78% of all Catholics do not identify themselves as being, "Born Again". Nor do 51% of all Methodists, 55% of all Presbyterians,

63% of all Lutherans, 29% of all Adventists and 29% of all Restorationists see themselves as "Born Again". These folks will not see the kingdom of God because they are not, "Born Again" by their own admission.

So, What Does It Mean To Be, "Born Again"?

To be "Born Again" is to undergo a "spiritual birth", or a regeneration of the human spirit by the power of the Holy Spirit. This is contrasted with the physical birth everyone experiences. It refers to being converted to a personal faith in Christ which causes the new birth to occur. It requires repentance from personal sin and accepting Jesus as Lord and Savior.

This report shows clearly that many of those who claim Christianity have fallen away from its roots and slipped off its foundation which is Christ. They still dwell in darkness and live in the flesh supporting a religious but carnal lifestyle.

The point is, they have fallen away or never knew true faith, much less the importance of practicing the Lordship of Christ.

Why Should We Make Jesus Lord Over Our Life?

When we truly are "Born Again" we want to please God. Our entire experience is based upon repentance. We openly admit to God that we have fallen short of his righteousness and are sorry for all the sin and rebellion we have participated in. Some of us would admit that we did a very bad job of managing our own lives. We didn't have the foresight to make good decisions. We got caught up into demonic snares like drugs, alcohol, immoral sex, hate, and all the other evils of this world. In short, we made a mess of things and now are in need of a Savior that will come and take charge and straighten things out.

Benefits of Jesus As Our Lord And Savor

No Worrying…You don't have to worry about everything that comes up. Our trust is in Jesus. He will handle it.

Divine Power … to overcome bad habits and temptations.

Peace of Mind… because you now can rest, knowing that all things will work together for your good. (Romans 8:28)

Ringside Seat… in the battle of the ages as the Lord himself fights your battle with evil forces. (Psalm 27:1-3)

Enhanced Relationship… with Christ because you are walking closer to him and listening for His voice.

Personal Satisfaction… knowing that you are pleasing the Lord and honoring him.

Special Revelation… as the Holy Spirit gives you words to say and a course of actions to take in troubling situations.

Answered Prayer…Being in tune with the Holy Spirit brings answers to our prayers in a clear and understandable way.

The idea of the Lordship of Christ… it does not consist of one act of obedience but rather is measured by the sum of our obedience, and it cannot be accomplished in our own strength or power, but by the power available to us by the indwelling Holy Spirit. We are strongest when we are relying on him (2 Corinthians 12:10).

It's All or Nothing

Being a Christian is no joke. It is not a, "get out of jail free" card in some quasi-monopoly game of life. It is an all or nothing situation. You cannot live life with one foot in a world of carnality and the other in the spiritual realm. Jesus said, "He that is not with me is against me; and he that gathers not with me scatters abroad. Matthew 12:30 There is no in-between. No neutral ground. We are with him or against him.

There are lots of folks that play church, talking the talk, acting as though they understand but fail in the final analysis. It's like what Jesus said to the scribes and Pharisees of his day, "Woe to you, scribes and Pharisees, hypocrites! For you clean the outside of the cup and of the dish, but inside they are full of robbery and self-indulgence." NASV Matthew 20:25 We do not want to be like them.

Christianity is an absolute surrender to God. Jesus said, "For whosoever will save his life shall lose it: and whosoever will lose his life for my sake shall find it." Matthew 16:25 He also said, "If any *man* will come after me, let him deny himself, and take up his cross, and follow me." Matthew 16:24

It is high time that we, you and me and all the other believers, sell out to Jesus and surrender to his will. He will not let us down. He is a loving God, compassionate, caring and gentle in all his ways. His Lordship is in our best interest.

Remember, he is Lord of all, whether we like it or not. However, he gives us a choice to get on board with his plan or fall by the wayside. He takes no prisoners.

CHAPTER TEN:
TODAY'S MANNA FROM HEAVEN

Waiting for the Lord to return requires continual nourishment. We will need spiritual food to keep our spirit man strong and healthy as we travel through this wilderness world.

God rained down "Manna" from heaven to feed the children of Israel while they were in route from Egypt to the land of Canaan. This was just after God opened the Red Sea and the Jews crossed over to safety on dry land.

Their 400+ years in bondage were over and they were heading to the "Promised Land" that God gave Abraham. They gave up the fleshpots, cool water and abundance of food, trusting God to provide for them as they entered and traveled through the wilderness.

This is a picture of us leaving the bondage of sin to walk with the Lord. We end up in our own private wilderness heading for the presence of God and the victorious Christian life promised by Jesus in John 10:10.

It is believed that there were over 2 1/2 million in the caravan that Moses led out of Egypt. This would include men and women and children. They all left Egypt with hope, faith, and trust in God and were strongly committed to holding on until they made it to their Promised Land.

The Wilderness

"And they took their journey from Elim, and all the congregation of the children of Israel came unto the wilderness of Sin, which is between Elim and Sinai, on the fifteenth day of the second month after their departing out of the land of Egypt. And the whole congregation of the children of Israel murmured against Moses and Aaron in the wilderness:

And the children of Israel said unto them, Would to God we had died by the hand of the Lord in the land of Egypt, when we sat by the flesh pots, and when we did eat bread to the full; for ye have brought us forth into this wilderness, to kill this whole assembly with hunger."

Manna From Heaven

"Then said the Lord unto Moses, Behold, I will rain bread from heaven for you; and the people shall go out and gather a certain rate every day, that I may prove them, whether they will walk in my law, or no."

"And it shall come to pass, that on the sixth day they shall prepare that which they bring in; and it shall be twice as much as they gather daily. And Moses and Aaron said unto all the children of Israel, at even, then ye shall know that the Lord hath brought you out from the land of Egypt:" Exodus 16:1-6

This Manna was not only God's provision to keep the people alive but it was also a sign that proved that God was really leading them. It was a miracle that would show the Israelites God's love and mercy.

God made sure that the Manna was seen as an authentic miracle by raining it down from heaven. He did this for 40 years.

Manna looked like coriander seed and tasted like wafers made with honey (Exodus 16: 31). When the Israelites saw it, they asked each other, "What is it?" This led to the name "manna, " "what?"

It came each morning, except on the Sabbath day. It could be collected each day for that day alone, and only as much as could be eaten in one day. If a person tried to collect more than needed or to store the manna for future needs, it would grow wormy and foul (v. 20).

In this way, it was impossible for the Israelites to evade total dependence on God or to use the manna greedily for personal gain. Miraculously, the manna could be preserved on the sixth day and eaten on the Sabbath, and it was not to be found on the Sabbath morning (vv. 22-29).

The Rebellious

Eventually, rebellious Israelites grew tired of the manna and regretted the day they were delivered from their bondage (Num 11:6). They came to detest the manna and longed instead for the rich foods of Egypt (v. 5). But God continued to give the Israelites a steady supply of manna during their forty years of desert wanderings.

When Joshua and the children of Israel crossed the Jordan River and entered the Promised Land at Gilgal, they celebrated the Passover and ate the produce of the land. On that day, the manna ceased, again illustrating its miraculous provision (Joshua 5:12).

The Purpose of The Manna

The purpose of the Manna was to test Israel's faith, to humble them, and to teach them that "Man does not live on bread alone but on every word that comes from the mouth of the Lord" (Deut. 8:3,16). A hungry Jesus used this quote to refuse Satan's suggestion that he turn stones into bread (Matt 4:4). Like the Israelites in the desert, Jesus was totally dependent on the provisions of his heavenly Father while in the wilderness of temptation (Matt 4:11).

"Bread of Life"
A Metaphor of Jesus

The people in Jesus' day misunderstood the significance of the manna. They longed for a physical miracle, like the manna, which would prove to them that Jesus' words were true (John 6:31). But Jesus wanted his disciples to seek for the bread of heaven that gives life to the world, instead of physical bread to satisfy their appetites. When they asked, "From now on give us this bread, " he answered, "**I am the bread of life"** (vv. 32-35).

To the church in Pergamos, Jesus encouraged faithfulness by promising that true believers would receive "hidden manna" to eat (Rev 2:17). Just as Moses' manna brought with it physical blessing, so this heavenly reward will bring eternal life. (Contributed by William T. Arnold…Baker's Evangelical Dictionary).

Manna Was The, "Bread of Heaven"

Manna was the "Bread of Heaven" it was a metaphor or picture of Jesus. He said this about himself.

"I am the Bread of Life" (John 6:35) is one of the seven "I AM" statements of Jesus.

Jesus used the same phrase "I AM" in seven declarations about himself. In all seven, he combines "I AM" with tremendous metaphors, which expressed his, saving relationship toward the world. All appear in the book of John.

John 6:35 says, "I am the bread of life; whoever comes to me shall not hunger, and whoever believes in me shall never thirst."

A Basic Dietary Item

Bread is considered a staple food—i.e., a basic dietary item. A person can survive a long time on only bread and water. Bread is such a basic food item that it becomes synonymous for food in general. We even use the phrase "breaking bread together" to indicate the sharing of a meal with someone.

Bread also plays an integral part of the Jewish Passover meal. The Jews were to eat unleavened bread during the Passover feast and then for seven days following as a celebration of the exodus from Egypt.

When the Jews were wandering in the desert for 40 years, God rained down "bread from heaven" to sustain the nation (Exodus 16:4).

All of this plays into the scene being described in John, chapter 6, when Jesus used the term "bread of life." He was trying to get away from the crowds to no avail. He had crossed the Sea of Galilee, and the crowd followed him. After some time, Jesus inquires of Philip how they're going to feed the crowd. Philip's answer displays his "little faith" when he says they don't have enough money to give each of them the smallest morsel of food.

Finally, Andrew brings to Jesus a boy who had five small loaves of bread and two fish. With that amount, Jesus miraculously fed the people with lots of food to spare.

Afterward, Jesus and his disciples cross back to the other side of Galilee. When the crowd sees that Jesus has left, they follow him again.

Jesus takes this moment to teach them a lesson. He accuses the crowd of ignoring his miraculous signs and only following him for the "free meal." Jesus tells them in John 6:27,

"Do not labor for the food that perishes, but for the food that endures to eternal life, which the Son of Man will give to you. For on him God the Father has set his seal."

In Other Words

In other words, they were so enthralled with the food, they were missing out on the fact that their Messiah had come. So, the Jews ask Jesus for a sign that he was sent from God (as if the miraculous feeding and the walking across the water weren't enough).

They tell Jesus that God gave them manna during the desert wandering.

Jesus responds by telling them that they need to ask for the true bread from heaven that gives life. When they ask Jesus for this bread, Jesus startles them by saying,

"I am the bread of life; whoever comes to me shall not hunger, and whoever believes in me shall never thirst."

A Phenomenal statement!

This is a phenomenal statement!

First, by equating himself with bread, Jesus is saying he is *essential* for life.

Second, the life Jesus is referring to is not physical life, but eternal life. Jesus is trying to get the Jews thinking of the physical realm and into the spiritual realm. He is contrasting what he brings as their Messiah with the bread he miraculously created the day before. That was physical bread that perishes. He is spiritual bread that brings eternal life.

Third, and very important, Jesus is making another claim to deity. This statement is the first of the "I AM" statements in John's Gospel.

The Phrase "I AM"

The phrase "I AM" is the covenant name of God (Yahweh, or YHWH), revealed to Moses at the burning bush (Exodus 3:14). The phrase speaks of self-sufficient existence (or what theologians refer to as *"aseity"*), which is an attribute only God possesses. It is also a phrase the Jews who were listening would have automatically understood as a claim to deity.

Fourth, notice the words "come" and "believe." This is an invitation for those listening to place their faith in Jesus as the Messiah and Son of God.

The Invitation

This invitation to come is found throughout John's Gospel. Coming to Jesus involves making a choice to forsake the world and follow Jesus. Believing in Jesus means placing our faith in him that he is who he says he is, that he will do what he says he will do, and that he is the only one who can.

Fifth, there are the words "hunger and thirst." Again, it must be noted that Jesus isn't talking about alleviating physical hunger and thirst.

The key is found in another statement Jesus made, back in his Sermon on the Mount. In Matthew 5:6, Jesus says,

"Blessed are those who hunger and thirst for righteousness, for they shall be satisfied."

When Jesus says those who come to him will never hunger and those who believe in him will never thirst, he is saying he will satisfy our hunger and thirst to be made righteous in the sight of God.

Modern Day Use of Manna A Spiritual Application

Jesus said he was the "Bread of Life" and the "Bread" that came down from heaven. We know from John chapter one that Jesus was pre-existent as God and became man so he could be our Savior. Thus the, "Bread of Heaven" was and is the Word that became flesh and dwelt among us. (John 1:14)

If we go to the Word of God every day, like the Old Testament saints went out to gather Manna, we would be filled with all the spiritual nutrients necessary to live in the wilderness of this world.

The Bible is the Manna of our day. It took hundreds of years to grow and it is for everyone. We need only to open the Bible and gather the spiritual food (Bread) that God has waiting for us.

Never Too Much

I know that some will say, just like the Israelites in the wilderness, I am tired of this Manna. The literal Manna may have become unappealing after eating it for 40 years. However, the Bread from heaven" does not get old; does not lose its flavor and will not cause you to wish for something else that is more satisfying.

The "Heavenly Manna" is the word of God and when it is sent from heaven it accomplishes all that God intended it to do.

"So shall my word be that goes forth out of my mouth: it shall not return unto me void, but it shall accomplish that which I please, and it shall prosper in the thing whereto I sent it." Isaiah 545:11

We can trust that when God sends us Manna from heaven, it will arrive safely and be a blessing to us.

The provision of Manna was to sustain the children of God while traveling in the wilderness. The trip was only about 3 1/2 days. However, because of the rebellion and idol worship in the camp, God chose to keep them in a state of wandering for 40 years until a new generation could emerge.

The new generation, at the direction of God, went into the "Promised Land" and took it for themselves. Once they settled and were able to grow their own food, the Manna stopped falling from heaven. This suggests several things that can apply to the Christian walk for faith. They are:

The Manna was only temporary. It was never given as a 40-year provision. It ended up being just that but it was not planned that way.

The purpose of the Manna was to teach faith and dependency to the newly founded nation. It was a way to test their faith on an on-going basis.

Manna from heaven is a metaphor for Spiritual sustenance but it cannot go beyond the physical realm… whereas the "Bread of Life" is an eternal provision.

The wilderness is a place of wandering for those that reject God's love and guidance. The rebellious go into it but never come out.

The Manna was a sign from God that proved to the people that God was really leading them.

We, like Old Testament saints, have seen the promises of God afar off and now consider ourselves strangers and pilgrims in the earth. Hebrews 11:13… We too are on our way to the "Promised Land."

The, "Bread of Life" being a type of Spiritual Manna, is designed to sustain us in a wilderness-world as we walk in the Spirit; fight the good fight of faith and stand fast in the liberty that we have in Christ…until we see Jesus, face to face and are welcomed home by God, our Heavenly Father. When that happens, the need for Manna will be no longer because we will have arrived at our destination.

The Bible is the Manna of our day. We will starve and even live life in a weakened state of mind without it. It is our only source by which we can mature in Christ. It is the Manna that helps us to discover the promises of God, and commune with the Holy Spirit.

"Thy word have I hid in mine heart, that I might not sin against thee." Psalm 119:11 kjv

CONCLUSION

We look for the coming of our Lord, believing that he will appear within our lifetime. We watch for signs and think about what it would be like to be caught up together in the clouds to be with him. We wonder how that all will happen and what it will look like on the evening news.

Questions will arise in our minds like, "What will it really be like?" "How will we survive?" "Will I really be spared from the wrath to come or will I suffer, not understanding why?"

How is it that I am here on earth at this time and in this place? Do I shout, "The Sky Is Falling! The Sky Is Falling! like Chicken Little or do I keep quiet and let destiny take its course.?

There is a lot to ponder and much to consider. I can hear the voice of the Lord telling me to comfort myself and those around me with the hope of his return. How can my prayers help those who reject the truth to live a carnal lifestyle?

I know that Jesus is coming soon. My spirit hungers for the presence of God and to be free from evil thoughts and practices. I cannot claim any betterment over those who are lost and heading towards eternal destruction. I only know and believe that God is good and he will judge me and the rest of the inhabitants of earth in righteousness.

I wait for that day with anticipation and even joy, knowing that those who are evil and bent on hurting others will suddenly disappear into an eternal lake of fire. I look forward to the time when I will see my brethren in Christ stand beside me in white robes of righteousness as we sing praises to the "Most High" and glorify the name of Jesus together.

I have written what I believe and have documented all with Biblical references so the truth can clearly be seen and heard. May my voice be as one crying in the wilderness of our day. Send it forth, oh Lord, on the winds of destiny to the hearts of all who need to hear.

ABOUT THE AUTHOR
JOHN MARINELLI

Rev. Marinelli is an ordained minister, He has formed and been pastor of one church in Wisconsin and was the pastor of another in Alabama. He has also been a youth minister and evangelism director over the years.

Rev. Marinelli has authored several other books including: "Original Story Poems", "The Art of Writing Christian Poetry," "Pulpit Poems," "Moonlight & Mistletoe," "The Mysterious Stranger," "With Eagles Wings," "Mysteries & Miracles," "It Came To Pass," Why Do The Righteous Suffer," "Believer's Handbook of battle Strategies." "Hidden In Plain Sight" "The End of The World, From The Beginning, Shadows in the Light of a Pale Moon," "Mister Tugboat" "An Elephant Named Clyde" "Morning Reign" "Times Past But Not Forgotten" "How To Be Happy" and "How To Have A Victorious Christian Life."(www.marinellichristianbooks.com)

John is an accomplished Christian poet. He also dabbles in songwriting, likes to play chess, sings karaoke and goes fishing now and then. He lives in north central Florida where he enjoys a retired lifestyle with his wife and two collies.

GALLERY OF ENCOURAGING CHRISTIAN POEMS

AGREEING WITH GOD

We speak of things that are not,
Believing in them as though they were,
Because our Heavenly Father spoke them first,
Sending them to us in promises that never blur.

We take Him at His Word,
And listen to all He has to say.
We wrap each promise around our souls,
Until what was spoken becomes our day.

We will agree with the Lord,
Trusting that He knows best.
For only His awesome power,
Can provide our souls with rest.

"As it is written, I have made thee a father of many nations, before Him who he believed, even God who quickens the dead and calls those things that be not as though they were" Romans 4:17

Like Abraham, we also have a destiny that God has spoken into our lives. He calls it forth before it exists. Like Abraham, we are to believe, even against hope, that what God said will indeed come to be. (Romans 4:18).

ARM'S LENGTH

I hold the world at arm's length,
That its choices do not interfere.
While it does its own thing,
I watch and wait over here.

My steps must not go that way,
For it's not where I need to be.
The Lord has shown me the path,
That will lead me to my destiny.

The call of the world is strong
And pulls at me now and then.
But I know that way
Is full of sorrow and sin.

I must move on in life
Beyond their beckoning call.
It's the right thing to do,
So I do not stumble or fall.

I will not be swayed or misled
By family, friends or business deal.
Their secret thoughts are not mine,
To consider, to admire or feel.

So I keep the world at "Arm's Length"
As I journey through this life.
My faith in Jesus keeps me strong,
As I walk in His glorious light.

"Love not the world, neither the things that are in the world. If any man loves the world, the love of the Father is not in him. For all that is in the world, the lust of the flesh, the lust of the eyes and the pride of life, is not of the Father, but of the world. And the world passes away and the lust thereof: But he that doeth the will of God abides forever. I John 2:15-17

It is more important to know God and to follow after Him, than to become entangled in life's lustful traps: for if we were to gain the whole world and lose our own soul, how terrible would that be?

DON'T WORRY

Don't worry about tomorrow.
You did that yesterday.
Go on with your life
And remember always to pray.

Ask and it shall be given to you,
But this great truth you already know.
Rejoice and be happy, why? Because…
Your harvest comes from what you sow.

I will say it again and even more,
Until it becomes very very clear.
Tomorrow will take care of itself,
But worry is another word for fear.

Now here's what I want you to do.
Trust in the Lord and be of good cheer.
Drop the worry from your vocabulary
And cast out that demon of fear.

Worry is the flipside of faith. If you are walking in faith, you are free from worry. Why, because faith hopes in God and trusts that he will be there to meet your need.

TWO HOUSES

We built our homes together,
Mine upon a Rock and his in the sand.
He thought his would be all right,
But he was a foolish man.

God's wisdom showed me the way.
And what I needed to do,
But my foolish neighbor,
Never had a clue.

Then the rains came,
And the winds began to blow.
The storms beat upon our homes,
And we had nowhere to go.

We built our homes together,
My neighbor and me.
Mine is still there upon the Rock,
But his ceased to be.

Wise men and fools both suffer,
The storms that befall mankind.
But those who trust in Jesus
Will always stand the test of time.

Foundation is everything. If you build your life on the Word of God, it will last forever. That's why we strive to be obedient to the will of God. We want his destine and his blessings, no matter what the world system thinks or does.

CLUTTER

Clutter keeps the mind confused,
As images dance through the night.
Lost among those unimportant thoughts,
Are the dreams that once shined bright.

An endless parade of fear and doubt,
Crowds the mind to destroy our day.
Ever soaring on the wings of the soul,
Until it has formed an evil array.

But clutter is by one's choice,
Of those who dance to its beat.
Better to face imaginations' due
Than to fall into utter defeat.

Be Quiet!!! Is our spirit's desperate cry,
As we call upon the name of the Lord.
Silence is our heart's desired prayer,
Until our minds are again restored.

"Keep thy heart with all diligence: for out of it are the issues of life" Proverbs 4:23

We make the final choices in life that either lead us astray or closer to the Lord. We chose what enters our hearts and fills our minds. May we always choose the path of righteousness and the way of peace.

THE LORD'S LITTLE TWO BY FOUR

God has a little 2' X 4'
That rest on heaven's windowsill.
He uses it now and then,
When we stray from His will.

Sometimes we need a good "Bap";
With the Lord's little 2' X 4'
To knock out the confusion,
And help us to desire Him more.

The Lord's little 2' X 4'
Is what we sometimes need,
To get our thinking straight,
And keep our focus indeed.

The Lord's little 2' X 4'
Is fashioned from life's every trial,
So we do not stray from His will,
Or fall into an ungodly lifestyle.

"My son, despise not the chastening of the Lord; neither be weary of His correction: for whom the Lord loves, He corrects; even as a father his son, in whom he delights." Proverbs 3:11 & 12

It is a good thing to be corrected by God. We should not fear His rebuke for it is not His wrath, but rather a blessing from His love that keeps us moving on towards maturity.

I FIND MYSELF IN GOD

I find myself in God.
He is my, "Everything"
I know that He is Lord,
My Life, My Hope, My King.

I find myself in God,
Not the ways of Sin.
Nor do I look to others,
To know who I really am.

I find myself in God,
To whom I bow on bended knee.
He alone is my joy and strength
And where I want to be.

"For we are His workmanship, created in Christ Jesus unto good works, which God hath before ordained, that we should walk in them" Ephesians 2:10

Knowing that we are created in Christ Jesus gives us confidence to walk in Christ, as He walked, along a pathway of good works. It is our joy and pleasure to be like Him. In Him we move and live and have our being.

"I AM" THERE

"I AM" There,
At the end of your broken dreams,
Before the sun rises over your day,
Prior to those tear-filled streams.

"I AM" There,
Down that road of despair,
When all appears to be lost,
And no one seems to care.

"I AM" There,
Over all of life's twists and turns,
When tomorrow is all but gone,
And when you are full of concerns.

"I AM" There,
Sayeth the Lord of Host,
To bring you hope and peace,
And the power of My Holy Ghost.

"I AM" There,
To be sure you make it through,
In the midst of every trial,
To bless your life and deliver you.

"I Am" There

"All power is given unto me in heaven and earth. Go ye therefore and teach all nations, baptizing them in the name of the Father, and of the Son, and of the Holy Ghost: Teaching them to observe all things, whatsoever I have commanded you: and lo, I am with you always, even unto the end of the world." Mathew 28:18-20

The Lord is with us always. He never leaves our side, even when we leave His. In every situation, He is there. It's time to count on His presence and trust in His care.

SO LISTEN UP

I write this verse that all should know.
What I have to say is like a seed, ready to grow.
So listen up to all I have to say.
It could be the very blessing your heart needs today.

God has not given you a spirit of fear.
Instead, He has offered to dry up every tear.
He really loves you, even though you often fail.
His love and mercy follows you,
Enabling you to be the head and not the tail.
So do not worry or even fret.
That's why Jesus paid sin's awful debt.
Now go on in life to discover its victory
Knowing that Jesus has indeed set you free.

"For God hath not given us the spirit of fear: but of Power and of Love and a sound mine" II Timothy 1:7

There is nothing to fear except fear itself and that spirit has been defeated on the cross. We now have the Spirit of power and love and a sound mind. He will never leave us or forsake us. We are truly free.

WINNING THE BATTLE

We must use the Word of God
To calm emotions that fray.
For the enemy never sleeps,
Until he has led us astray.

So when your emotions overflow
With feelings like depression and fear.
Know this! If you dwell in that place,
You invite the enemy to draw near.

When your emotions rage
With fiery darts aglow,
Stand in the power of the Lord,
Against its awful woe.

And if you get confused
And lost in the storm,
Put your thoughts on trial,
Rejecting all but heaven born.

You can win the battle
That rages within your soul.
By casting down imaginations,
And breaking Satan's hold.

Remember to focus on Jesus,
Holding the world at arm's length.
Lift up your head above the trial,
And the Lord will give you strength.

"For the weapons of our warfare are not carnal but mighty, through God, to the pulling down of strongholds: casting down imaginations and every high thing that exalts itself against the knowledge of God, and bringing into captivity every thought to the obedience of Christ." II Corinthians 10:3-5 The battle is in our minds and we win by putting our thoughts on trial and casting out all that oppose the knowledge of God. This is true victory.

THE LIGHTHOUSE

A lighthouse is a blessing,
To the ships that toss in the sea.
For it shows them the way,
Until they can clearly see.

The rage of an angry storm,
Cannot hide its brilliant light.
Nor can its awesome furry,
Rule as an endless night.

Jesus is the lighthouse,
For those who have gone astray.
The light of His love,
Offers a new and living way.
Jesus is the lighthouse,
When fear and sickness rage.
The light of His love,
Gives hope in difficult days.

So trust in the Lord,
And look for His light.
He alone is "The Lighthouse",
That guides you through the night.

"I am the Way, the Truth, and the Life. No man cometh to the Father but by me" John 14:6

Life holds many dark nights that are full of unexpected storms. Only a deep abiding faith in Jesus Christ will get us through. He is the light of the world. His light keeps us from falling into confusion, sorrow, sickness and demonic oppression.

THE WAY MAKER

Only Jesus can make a way,
Through the difficulties of life.
He alone is Lord and King,
Over life's sorrows and strife.

He is the "Way Maker,"
When there is no visible way.
He will make the way known,
As though it were the light of day.

He will make a way,
For those of humble heart.
He will clear away the rubble,
Restoring what Satan broke apart.
Jesus is the "Way Maker,"
A friend to all who are lost.
He has made the way,
Paying sin's incredible cost.

The way to the Maker,
Is through His only Son.
He alone is the "Way Maker,"
Until life's battles are won.

"Let not your heart be troubled. Ye believe in God, believe also in me. In my father's house are many mansions: If it were not so, I would have told you. I go to prepare a place for you. And if I go and prepare a place for you, I will come again, and receive you unto myself, that where I am, there ye may be also." John 14: 1-3

The Lord is prepared for any emergency. He knows the beginning from the end and has gone before us to prepare a way that we can follow until we see Him face to face.

STINKING THINKING

Stinking thinking, they say,
Is bad for your health.
For it frustrates life's goals,
And denies happiness and wealth.

A right perspective is important,
As we think about everything.
It will either bring us down,
Or cause us to shout and sing.

What we think about these days,
Really does affect our life.
It can cause us to overflow with Joy,
Or fall into depression and strife.

So don't let your thinking,
Stink all the way up to heaven.
Stand in faith before God,
And get rid of that negative leaven.

"Then Jesus said unto them, take heed and beware of the leaven of the Pharisees and the Sadducees" Mathew 16:6

Someone once said, "We are what we think" The Bible says, "As a man thinks, so is he" It is important to concentrate our thinking of those things that are of good report, pure, honest and that will keep us clean of heart.

WISE MEN STILL SEEK HIM

Wise men still seek Him
Who appeared so long ago.
They come now by grace
Through faithful hearts aglow.

Wise men still seek Him
For He is their "Bread of Life."
A sustaining inner strength
Through times of sorrow or strife.

Wise men still seek Him
The Christ of Calvary.
God's only begotten Son
Crucified as Sin's penalty.

Wise men still seek Him
Jesus, God in human array.
King of kings & Lord of lords
Born to earth on Christmas Day.

"Now when Jesus was born in Bethlehem of Judea in the days of Herod the king, behold, there came wise men from the east to Jerusalem, saying, where is he that is born king of the Jews? For we have seen his star in the east and are come to worship him" Mathew 2:1-2

Seeking Jesus is the wisest thing any man, woman or child can do and when we find Him, it is our privilege to bow down and worship Him. This is our journey, our destiny and our life while on this earth.

THE ANGELS CRY HOLY

The Angels cry "Holy,"
While sorrow fills the land.
For God's Judgment Day,
Is to come upon every man.

The Angels cry "Holy,"
While mankind goes astray,
Rejecting the love of God,
To follow his own precarious way.

The Angels cry "Holy,"
Knowing the terror of the Lord,
When all who dwell in sin,
Will suddenly be destroyed.

The Angels cry "Holy,"
Waiting for all things new,
Born of the Holy Spirit,
When God's Judgment is through.

The Angels cry "Holy,"
"Holy is the Lamb,"
Waiting for the children of God,
To join "The Great I AM"

"And one cried unto another and said, "Holy, Holy, Holy, is the Lord of host: the whole earth is full of his glory" Isaiah 6:3

We serve a Holy God that deserves our reverence and homage. The angels know this and worship Him, but man, because of sin, has no real concept of his own creator.

A HIGHWAY CALLED "HOLINESS"

He places my feet on
A highway called "Holiness,"
That led my soul
To the throne of God.

Amidst the cheers of angels,
I walk, wearing His holy gown.
Onward towards heaven's throne,
While evil cast its awful frown.

My eyes were opened
That I might see.
Both the good and the evil,
That sought after me.

I walk the highway-Holiness
That crosses all of time.
Towards the throne of God,
Leaving this world behind.

"And an highway shall be there, and a way, and it shall be called, the way of holiness; the unclean shall not pass over it; but it shall be for those: the wayfaring men, though fools, shall not err therein. No lion shall be there, nor any ravenous beast shall go up thereon, it shall not be found there, but the redeemed shall walk there. And the redeemed of the Lord shall return, and come to Zion with songs and everlasting joy upon their heads: They shall obtain joy and gladness, and sorrow and sighing shall flee away. " Isaiah 35:8-10

What a privilege to walk the highway of Holiness. It is prepared especially for us, the redeemed, and it is protected from the errors of fools and the snarl of beast and especially the roar of the lion.

CALL UPON THE LORD

When your burdens overwhelm you,
Like a mighty raging sea.
Call upon the Lord, Jesus,
And He will set you free

When your heartaches are many,
And life is difficult to understand.
Call upon the Lord, Jesus.
He will come and hold your hand.

When your friends reject you,
Because you follow after Him,
Call upon the Lord, Jesus.
And keep yourself from sin.

When you fall into depression,
As though it were a giant pit.
Call upon the Lord, Jesus,
Who will restore your joyful wit.

When you're saddened by the day
Feeling lost and all alone.
Call upon the Lord, Jesus,
Who will make His way known.

When you are weary and heavy laden,
Tired from life's many tests.
Call upon the Lord, Jesus,
Who is sure to give you rest.

"Hear my cry; oh God, attend unto my prayer. From the end of the earth,

I will cry unto thee, when my heart is overwhelmed: Lead me to the rock that is higher than I." Psalms 61:1-2

Calling upon the Lord in stressful times is o.k. He wants us to cry to Him and then to trust in Him to watch over His Word to perform it on our behalf.

IT CAME TO PASS

Things often come to pass,
But seldom do they ever last.
They come into our busy day,
For awhile, then pass away.

We hear their voices, loud and clear,
As they arrive and while they are here.
They speak both joy and misery,
Some to you and some to me.

We say, "It came to pass,"
Or say, "It happened so fast."
Down life's beaten path,
Comes both love and wrath.

So say goodbye to sad and blue.
To all that is now troubling you.
For things will come, only to pass,
But God's love will always last.

"And it came to pass in those days…" Luke2:1

These are the times of our lives. We live them, some for good and some for not so good. One thing is for sure, that which comes our way, comes only to pass on by. It is not what happens that is so important, but rather what we do with what we are faced with.

Trusting in the Lord and seeking His guidance will always conquer that which comes to pass.

THE WHOSOEVER SCENARIO

The "Whosoever" is who so ever,
Not who so won't, can't or will not.
The story is as clear as a sunny day.
God offers a new and living way.

But only those who engage "free will"
To choose life, faith and obedience,
Will find salvation for their souls,
And be cleansed and made whole.

We do the choosing: to accept or deny.
That is how God set it up to be.
He made the call to life's "Whosoever",
That they could live abundantly.

"For God so loved the world, that he gave his only begotten son, that whosoever believeth in him, should not perish but have everlasting life." John 3:16

We are the "Whosoever" in John 3:16, that one day put his or her faith in Christ, believed in Him and now rest in the Lord's love and grace. We have the promise of God that He sent His Son so we could believe and have everlasting life. How great is that?

LITTLE PRISONS

Little prisons await the man with a lustful soul.
Bars of selfishness and pride create dungeons of icy cold.

Prisons of shame and jealousy fill the heart with utter despair.
Bars that separate from God and those that really care.

Stand back! While the doors are tightly closed;
Taking away your life, to wither as a dying rose.

Beware of those little prisons that trap the lustful soul.
Keep yourself free from sin through faith in the Christ of old.

Little prisons need not to be your fate.
It is your choice, Spirit or flesh to date.

"O Foolish Galatians, who hath bewitched you, that ye should not obey the truth, before whose eyes Jesus Christ hath been, evidently set forth, crucified among you? Are you so foolish? Having begun in the Spirit, are you now made perfect in the flesh?

We should always seek to dwell in the Spirit, that we would not emulate the deeds of the flesh. When we fall short, we create "little prisons" that keep us in confusion and away from the blessing of God. It's time to walk in the Spirit and break the prisons that so easily beset us.

REST MY CHILD

Rest my child, says the Lord.
Take thy peace and be restored.
I have provided, thy mouth to feed.
From the beginning, I knew your need.

Do not worry, fret or even fear,
For, my child, I am always near
To bless thy soul with love and grace,
To be with thee, face to face.

Come, my child, near to my throne.
Do not allow your faith to roam.
For those who will not believe
Can never find rest in times of need.

My Word shall see you through.
My grace I freely give to you
That you should rest, thy soul to keep,
Forever delivered from unbelief.

Resting in the Lord is the best way to stay happy. However, it requires faith and trust in God that he will be there for you when you need him. It's kind of neat to relax when fear and anxiety are knocking at your door.

A WHISPER IN THE WIND

There's a whisper in the wind
That lingers both day and night.
A champion of truth and justice,
By the power of His might.

A word in due season
That echoes from deep within.
A voice out of nowhere,
Reproving the world of sin.

Look there, in the street
And here, by the shores of the sea.
There's a whisper hidden in the wind;
A voice from eternity.

There's a calling from God.
His voice is hidden in the wind.
In a whisper, He speaks to our hearts
With the love and counsel of a friend.

Listen for the Whisper,
All who seek to know.
It is God's Holy Spirit
Telling you which way to go.

"And thine ears shall hear a word behind thee saying, This is the way, walk ye in it, when ye turn to the right hand and when ye turn to the left" Isaiah 30:21

The voice of the Lord is often a still small voice, yet always clear and it never brings confusion. His voice is like a whisper in the wind that brings a peaceful breeze to the heart. The joy of hearing His voice is to know His will and our destiny.

FRAGILE FLOWER RED

As a flower in earthen sod,
I bloom for thee, oh God.
To blossom with the turn of spring;
To be to you, a beautiful thing.

I lift my Fragile Flower Red
Upward from my earthen bed;
To draw light from God above,
Strength and peace and joy and love.

As a flower, I bloom for thee
That passersby may stop and see.
Your fragrance and beauty I am,
Flowered in grace as a man.

As a flower in earthen sod,
I bloom for thee, oh God.
Upward, I lift my head,
As a Fragile Flower Red.

"Be not conformed to this world, but be ye transformed, by the renewing of your mind, that ye may prove what is that good and acceptable and perfect will of God."

When we look to God as our source, we blossom, much like a flower that draws light from the sun. When we blossom, like a flower, we display the glory and beauty of our creator to all who care to stop and look. This is our divine destiny.

Other books by John Marinelli can be viewed and purchased at: www.marinellichristianbooks.com

www.ingramcontent.com/pod-product-compliance
Lightning Source LLC
Chambersburg PA
CBHW020427010526
44118CB00010B/457